The Serial Killing Nudist & Other Bizarre Tales

Pete Crow

Published by Trellis Publishing, 2021.

THE SERIAL KILLING NUDIST & OTHER BIZARRE TALES

First edition. July 5, 2021.

Copyright © 2021 Pete Crow.

ISBN: 979-8224676972

Written by Pete Crow.

THE SERIAL KILLING NUDIST & OTHER BIZARRE TALES

PETE CROW

AMY DECHANT

Passport To The Underworld?

Arrested in a nudist colony on suspicion of murder. Life probably cannot get much lower, or more bizarre, than this. But then, for Amy Dechant, life has often seemed littered with tribulations.

Amy was born in the post war boom of the late 1940s, in the state of New Jersey. But for her, the abundance of the fifties managed to pass her by. Childhood was not a great time for the young girl. At just nine years old, she was orphaned, and subsequently was brought up by her aunt and uncle. By the age of seventeen, Amy was married, the first of her two husbands a High School sweetheart.

But if love was not often a great success for the young woman, despite her slight frame and attractive appearance, then she did show a talent in other fields. Notably, as a businesswoman. Basing herself in the world of cleaning services, she showed a propensity to set up companies, grow them and then move on to larger, more successful enterprises. Such schemes did not make her a millionaire, but they gave her a financial independence as she was maturing through her thirties and beyond.

But, by the early 1990s, Amy was getting tired of life in chilly New Jersey. She longed for a more consistent climate, for a new home. Somewhere that her talent for business could be developed even further. But, where to go? Her friend, Claudia McClure, had an idea. She was now living in Las Vegas, Nevada, and thought this might provide an ideal location for Amy. She knew that her friend enjoyed a lively social life, was fond of a gamble or two at the poker table – and there are few places in the US more able to provide those kind of thrills than Las Vegas.

'She didn't know where she was going,' Claudia recalled later 'so I said "Why don't you come to Las Vegas. I think you'd love it here."'

Amy did, and at the age of 45 found that her friend was absolutely correct. 'Las Vegas was right for me it offered opportunity, it had a very good climate for small business.' She recalled. Not only was that climate right for her sun tan, right for her love of a night at the poker table, but it was also ideal for her business ventures.

There can be few cities in the world where the need for a good, reliable business in the field of cleaning is more pronounced than Las Vegas. Amy got her latest venture underway. Soon the contracts were flooding in. She needed to expand and took her friend Claudia on to work with her. But she needed even more staff, and next employed a man called Bobby Jones. Many who knew him had little time for Bobby. Police would later refer to him as a gopher; with all the independence of thought of such a creature. It soon became apparent that Bobby was in awe of his successful boss. That developing dependence would be something he would come to regret. Yet as good as her business skills were, and as successfully as she was flourishing in Las Vegas, that other side of Amy's life, the romantic one, was still a mess.

She entered into several relationships. None of them delivered stability, and frequently she would have a number of boyfriends at once.

Clifford L Linedecker is author of 'Blood in the Sand', a book chronicling the complex case of Amy Dechant. 'She was a natural businesswoman,' he said. 'She started one business after another and they were successful.

Yet Linedecker also identified that other side of her personality: 'While she was doing this she was manipulating one or two or three romantic situations and she managed to balance everything of once.' But it was a strain.

However, her business was going from strength to strength. She secured a contract at the Las Vegas airport, McCarran International, there to clean the private planes of the rich. Next, she won the right to clean the carpets and upholstery at the MGM in Las Vegas itself.

But it was when she was spending a night in a Las Vegas Casino, gambling at a Texas Hold 'Em poker table, that a chance meeting would send her life spiralling upwards until it reached an apex, and from there to plummet back down to earth.

It was the fall of 1995 and another player at the table had a notable appearance. Savagely large – weighing in at around three hundred pounds – was a quiet, round faced man. He was a little younger than Amy (three years, she would later discover) but looked ten years older. His hair was long, tied back in a pony tail and grey white. Bruce Weinstein was a man previously married, but now on his own. A man who seemed to take little care of his health and body. A man who was clearly a wealthy individual.

He and Amy struck up a conversation, and found they got along. They arranged to meet again, and the friendship strengthened. When Bruce introduced her to his five-year-old daughter, Jacqueline, the bond grew quickly. Soon, it would begin to turn from friendship to love. But Bruce had another less desirable side, beyond that of his excessive eating.

He was part of a family business, one established for many years with branches not only in Las Vegas but also California. It was not the most noble of organisations. Bruce Weinstein ran the Las Vegas branch of his family's gambling cartel. An illegal one, at that.

Bruce was building a large new home for himself. And he quickly persuaded Amy that she should move in with him. Once the mansion was complete, she sold her own condo – bought (with much pride) when she had established herself in Las Vegas.

Amy held mixed feelings about the move. She was fond of Bruce's children, fond of Bruce himself. But she was also an independent woman, a success in her own right with a burgeoning career and a thriving business of her own. She knew that there would be compromises if she gave up some of her freedom.

'I was having fun and making money and to be honest with you I didn't want things to change. I knew that if I moved in with Bruce things would change,' she said later. 'But he needed me.'

At the time she spoke those words, Amy was incarcerated in the Southern Nevada Women's Correctional Center; she ended her sentence with self-deprecating irony:

'I'm just a sucker for someone who needs me sometimes.'

The idea that Bruce needed Amy was shared by a number of people. The first impressions made on Bruce's mother, Sylvia White, were positive. She saw that Amy helped him to control his diet, to eat sensibly. The weight just fell off the large man. Twenty, thirty, forty pounds were lost. Claudia also noted the positive effect that Amy was having.

'I think she was the best thing that happened to him in a long time,' she said.

Bruce held a very close relationship with his mother. He would visit her every day; would telephone her in the morning. To have her approval of his new relationship meant a lot. To both of them.

'She was watching over what he ate, making sure he was eating properly. So, I thought that she cared for him and was taking care of him,' said Sylvia.

But if the caricature of the criminal mind with the close tie to his mother is too much of a cliché in this case, there is no doubt that Bruce sailed close to the wind. Paul Bigham was an LA Police officer involved in the investigation that would soon be needed. He noted the illegal nature of the Weinstein family gambling business but saw that it had always just operated below the interest of the law. It is a fine line for a busy police force to know whether to make the decision to watch, infiltrate and investigate an operation that, while illegal, didn't seem to be doing too much harm.

Amy, though, had discovered that maybe there was more to the dealings of the Weinstein family than the police were aware. 'Let's just say it had some very cruel collection methods and being in the business for twenty years, let's just say they were very good at it,' she observed.

But, facts are facts and supposition is supposition. There was no doubt that Amy's involvement in Bruce's life should have extended it. Should have reduced the risk of heart disease, of diabetes, of cancer that his excessive and poor-quality eating was rapidly increasing in his body.

Yet that good would, at least in the eyes of the authorities, soon change to become the worst kind of evil. As is so often the case with murder, there are very differing accounts of what happened in the late hours of July 5th 1996. The absolutes surrounding that long night are minimal, the circumstantial evidence manifold.

Bruce Weinstein was a creature of habit. His day would start early, and he would always be up and active by the time the gambling lines opened at 6.30am. He would check on these, then phone his mother. The end of the day would be as predictable as the beginning. Weinstein had few friends, those running the darker side of the gambling world in a city like Las Vegas rarely did. Not proper friends, anyway. He would perhaps take a turn at the tables in a casino on the strip – just as he was doing on the evening he met Amy – but it was rare that he was not home and in bed by 9.30 at night.

So, when by 8.30 on the morning of July 6th Sylvia had still not heard from her son, she was seriously worried. That anxiety was heightened by the fact that Jacqueline had spent the night with her grandmother. Bruce was besotted with his young daughter and would never fail to check that she was happy and well.

Sylvia could wait no longer. She phoned Amy, and the story she received did not satisfy her. Amy said that Bruce had gone out the night before with a friend, he had left at about 11.00 and that he might be back today, or he might join her on their planned trip to Lake Tahoe. She said that she was in the shower when the friend called so she did not know who it was, but that there was nothing to worry about in the arrangement. It did not ring true to Sylvia – going out on the spur of moment late at night was just not the kind of behaviour her son, so rigid in his routine, displayed.

She decided to head straight over to the house. She arrived to find Amy cleaning the stair carpet, rubbing at its deep white pile. At the bottom was a small collection of her son's belongings: his favourite sandals, it was rare that he did not wear them; his cell phone, a tool a bookie is never without; his wallet.

Sylvia's doubts were heightened, but Amy seemed as normal; relaxed, chatty and at ease. It was an elaborate performance hiding her true inner turmoil. When Bruce had not shown up by the next day, and had made no contact with his family, Sylvia feared the worse. Anybody associated with the gambling industry shared their world with unsavoury types. Somebody running an illegal outfit of the kind operated by Weinstein was even more exposed to the underworld. Sylvia feared that her son had been abducted, that a ransom note would appear at any moment, or a phone call she both wanted, because it said her son was still alive, and equally dreaded because it identified him as being in serious danger.

But when nothing was heard the next day either, Bruce's brother reported him as a missing person. The police were unimpressed. A forty something man, wealthy and well able to look after himself, not seen for just a little more than two days? He could be anywhere – a spur of the moment holiday; an admission to hospital for a condition he did not want to share; a twenty-four-hour bender or locked in one of the many casinos that graced The Strip. Most likely of all, he was shacked up in some hotel room with a woman – something he did not want his girlfriend or his mother to find out.

Details were taken, but nothing was done. There were many, many higher priorities with which the police department had to deal.

But after two more days, there was still no sign of Bruce. No communication, no message of any sort - welcome or not - had been received. In a state of complete anxiety his family hired a private investigator to try and find him. Michael Wysocki set to work immediately, starting with a detailed search of the Weinstein residence.

But he could find no sign of a struggle of any kind, no evidence of any blood – indeed absolutely nothing to suggest that Bruce Weinstein had done anything or had anything done to him that would contradict the words of his girlfriend. It seemed like the police were right, and there was no missing person here. The bookie might have disappeared, but there was no reason to suspect that he would not turn up again any time soon.

Yet still niggling away at the back of Wysocki's mind was the conviction from Weinstein's mother and brother that something had happened to their family member.

'They thought he was being held for ransom, that somebody had him,' the Private Investigator recalls.

Then, on top of this, was the fact that Weinstein had left his cell phone behind. To stop checking on the lines that fuelled his income would be so out of character for the creature of habit that it really raised concerns. Failing to contact his mother was also such inexplicable behaviour that Wysocki continued to search for clues. Then there was Amy. She seemed too relaxed about the entire matter. Too in control. Surely, after three days, four days, five days she would be exhibiting some evidence of uncertainty. Some worry or at least curiosity? She was claiming, after all, that while Bruce had left with the mysterious friend on the evening of the July 5th, they had been planning to meet in Lake Tahoe on the 6th. Now it was the 11th July. Yet Amy appeared totally unflustered about her boyfriend's whereabouts.

As she said, he was a bookie, used to handling large amounts of cash. In fact, he had created a home made safe in the bedroom. He had cut a section out of the wall, and behind it stuffed the takings he had made. Then, the security of the money was completed by pushing a chest of drawers in front of the cut-out section, the portion of wall put back in place.

There were frequently very substantial sums stored there. In fact, during the time in question, there was more than $100000. To Amy, this explained his failure to take his wallet. While he had left his American Express card behind, which was unusual, he was a man whose business dealings were frequently shady. Who was not to say that he had with him a significant amount of cash? Further, there are more ways to stay in touch with a business than through a cell phone? She gave off the aura of a person not at all concerned. It was a powerful performance, but as the days developed the cracks in it began to appear.

This was the point that Wysocki made the discovery that would change the case forever and see it escalate into a full-scale murder investigation. He was looking once more around the bedroom when he chanced to take another look at their bed. This time, he went to town, stripping it of sheets and pillows and flipping the mattress over. There he saw a deep hole, one whose edges were burned – just as would likely have occurred had it been made by a bullet.

It was the tipping point. Alongside the wallet, cell phone, change in behaviour and length of time Bruce had been away, the damage to the mattress provided the final clue that this was now a matter for the police. Wysocki reported his findings, and the police themselves now decided it was time to get involved.

They suspected Amy from the start. Although there was no blood visible in the house, forensic tests quickly showed up, in blue ultra violet light, that a body had been shot then dragged down the stairs and through to the garage. Amy was called in for questioning about a week after the police started their investigation, and Officer Paul Bigham explained how her behaviour struck officers as unusual. 'It was an unusual interview to say the least,' he said, 'Amy Dechant came to the interview with a collection of handwritten notes.' He went on to say that such behaviour was unique in his experience.

But Amy had her own, plausible explanation for attending the interview with notes. She was a very self-disciplined woman, somebody who in her business life always had matters sorted and organised. She had taken notes because she wanted to make sure that everything she needed to say was said; that nothing was missed in the stress of the occasion.

And what she actually did say threw the case wide open. Her story to Sylvia White had been only a fraction of the truth. According to her testimony there had been a visit while she was in the shower late in the evening of July 5th. But it was not a friend, rather four hitmen with associations to the Mob. Three had taken Bruce to the bedroom, while one had grabbed her from the shower, and loosely tied her up. She heard a shot, but her guard told her not to worry. 'We don't hurt women or children,' he said. But he promptly contradicted his reassurance, saying that if she mentioned what she had heard, both she and Bruce's young daughter Jacqueline would be killed. The mob-men ordered her to clear up the mess they made from moving the body. After that, she should say nothing. Not to anybody.

She told police that she was terrified the mob would carry out their threat, so she stayed quiet. They did not believe her. And nor did Weinstein's family. The woman who had seemed so good for Sylvia's son was now, she believed, the person responsible for his death. But in terms of evidence, the police had virtually nothing that was concrete. They did not even have proof that Bruce was dead. Amy was allowed to leave. Which she did, quickly.

And then, on August 11th several miles out of town a couple of hikers found a body buried under a pile of rocks and stones. It was quickly identified as that of Bruce Weinstein, and he had been shot in the chest. The police moved in to speak further to Amy, but she had gone. It was several weeks before a report came in from Maryland.

A speeding car had been stopped and the officer had made the link between the sought-after woman and the driver. Amy was returned to Nevada.

Police identified that she would have needed an accomplice, and soon evidence was pointing towards the gopher himself, Bobby Jones. Prosecutor Edward RJ Kane adopted the term to describe the weak-willed man. 'Jones was a gopher who did what any gopher would do,' he told TV's 'Snapped' investigative programme when it reported on the case some years later.

But evidence linking Jones to the crime was not easy to find. Although he would later get a five-year sentence for aiding and abetting the killing, the evidence against him was circumstantial. A friend had identified that Jones once held a gun similar to the one that had been used to complete the assassination. Jones had suddenly, inexplicably, come into a substantial amount of money. He had also left Las Vegas and moved to Mexico.

The evidence against Amy, too, was no more than circumstantial. She was arrested, spent a couple of months in remand while a substantial bail figure was set. But her lawyers argued successfully that the police had little on which to hold her. The bail was reduced to $5000, which she paid and left town. When she failed to turn up for a Grand Jury hearing a week later, she became a fugitive.

Amy knew that her case was getting a lot of media attention. The story of a bookie living on the edge of the law, a man rolling in money, murdered by, it would seem, his new girlfriend was one that appealed to the more sensationalist elements of the media. Indeed, Amy would soon appear on TV's 'America's Most Wanted' programme.

But she was a resourceful woman. She bought wigs and adopted disguises. She got herself a camper van in which she lived, travelling from place to place. Then, one night she was in Florida, looking for a place to rest up. She had been on the run, evading detection, for over a year by now. She saw a sign for a nudist camp and decided to go there.

Unfortunately for her, she was recognised by a guest and the police moved in to arrest her.

Inside her van was found the disguises, over $100000 in cash and research paperwork on the laws of extradition from various countries of the world. To police, it was further proof of her guilt. To run from the law when under suspicion of murder, or afraid of the mob, might be reasonable. But the research into extradition seemed too planned, too deliberate. Even for a woman as organised as Amy? To her, the reason that she fled was simple: 'I was just terrified, all those people were following me.

'I felt isolated, no one to turn to.'

But the arresting officer in Florida, Charles Frank Scavuzzo, did not believe her: 'She said she was trying to avoid the mob but, in my opinion, she was trying to avoid law enforcement,' he argued.

This time, no bail was granted. The trial generated massive interest, with a packed courtroom day after day. Yet still the data the prosecution garnered was purely circumstantial. And the defence believed that they had compelling counter evidence to present. They demonstrated that it would simply not be possible to carry out the killing, dispose of the body and, crucially, clean up all the blood of which police had found hidden forensic evidence in the time between Bruce returning from work, and Sylvia arriving the following morning. Even with help. But the prosecution too believed it held evidence on which the jury would convict. The District Attorney Edward Kane said: 'For somebody to panic and run just because they are under investigation for a homicide is one thing, to run with a potful of money, disguises – there's no way to explain that to a jury.'

With nothing more than speculation, the prosecution team claimed that Amy had had an argument with Bruce over money, and something had snapped within her. That was why she had killed her boyfriend. As simple as an argument over money.

And that was the story the jury believed. In October 1998 Amy Dechant was convicted and sentenced to two life terms in jail, without the possibility of parole. The story should have ended there, but another twist or two was still to play out in this extraordinary tragedy.

Amy Dechant continued to protest her innocence, and her attorney, Daniel Albregts, fought on. He believed a terrible miscarriage of justice had taken place, and that was down to the actions of the police and prosecutors. 'This wasn't an investigation with an eye towards who did it, but an investigation with an eye towards proving Amy had done it,' he argued. He claimed that police had not given any credence to the idea that she was running from both the police, whom she feared would lead to her false imprisonment *and* the mob. The consequences of running into this group were even worse than being caught by the authorities.

Albregts argued that the entire action of the prosecution side had been spent trying to force through a conviction, at any price, rather than find the truth. He continued to argue that not only did the police have no hard evidence on which to base their case, but they had no motive either.

Amy supported this: 'I had my own money, I was a very independent person. It is laughable to think I was a black widow.'

And as quickly as May 2000, just eighteen months after the conviction, the Supreme Court overturned it. A witness, a former member of the police department, had called the mob story a 'fairy-tale'; it was a term picked up again by the prosecution team later in the trial. The defence had objected, but the judge over-ruled them. Supreme Court judges decided that the term was prejudicial, and non-evidenced. The trial judge should have acted, but he did not. A retrial was ordered.

But before that could take place, Amy accepted a lesser charge which her attorney said did not represent a declaration of guilt. She was sentenced to 10 to 25 years. Her first parole came up in 2008 but was unsuccessful. The board required an admission of guilt which Amy was not prepared to give. But three years later she was released.

Now she lives on, entering her later years and rebuilding her life. As to what happened in 1996, whether Bruce Weinstein was killed in a fit of anger fuelled by an argument about money...or whether he had swum too far in the murky waters of the criminal underworld and got out of his depth – we can only speculate. Probably, the only person who knows the truth is Amy Dechant. And her account is clear.

DEADLY HOUSEWIFE JOYCE COHEN

LARRY MARAVICH

Rather like our adolescence, we look back on the 1980s with a mixture of affection and embarrassment. Yes, we were cooky then, wore our greed on our sleeves and dabbled in the high life if we were in a position to do so.

Yet rather like our adolescent selves, those Reagan years could be pretty horrible, somewhat selfish and at times unthinking. This is certainly a description that fits the lifestyle of Joyce Cohen and her husband Stanley during that decade.

They lived a lavish lifestyle in the upmarket Miami region of Coconut Grove. The greenest part of the city, luxury houses mix with verdant trees and shopping malls. Private schools abound almost as frequently as the wildlife scattering among the Jaguars and Porsches. Restaurants and nightclubs burst with big spenders and high livers. And back in the late 1970s and early to mid-1980s those party-goers included, on a regular basis, the Cohens.

Their own house, really Stanley's, was a monster of extravagance and excess. Set high a bluff, the many roomed mansion was in the wealthiest part of the most expensive zip code in the city. Built from coral, with handmade tiled floors, nothing could have stated 'success' as much as this status symbol home.

For Joyce Lemay (as she was back then), meeting Stanley represented a significant change in lifestyle. Her childhood had been deeply troubled. Sent from relative to relative, fostered by twenty-seven families and a victim of childhood sexual abuse as well as, it has to be said, emotional mistreatment, her Illinois upbringing had been one to forget. As much as she could, at least.

Moving into adulthood, things got no better. A failed marriage followed, and Joyce decided to look for a new start further south in Miami. She took a job undertaking secretarial duties for a property developer – a big one – during the boom building period of the mid-1970s. High rises, houses, flats and hotels were springing up in

Florida's tourist city like spots on the innocent face of a measle ridden baby.

Joyce noticed an older man hanging around the office, one who seemed to command the respect of other employees. Not a customer, co-worker or even manager, this man was in fact the top dog, Stanley Cohen himself. This self-made man held a passion for construction and a fine reputation in the industry. The construction company for whom Joyce worked as a secretary bore his initials, SAC, and the very young but life worn lady had clearly caught his eye. Stanley had, like many of the very richest of people in the industry, happened to set off in the construction business at just the right time. Moving south from Long Island, he caught the building bubble as it was growing at its fastest and reaped the rewards.

It was a whirl wind romance. For Joyce, there was a triple attraction. Not only was she won over by Stanley's charm and sophistication, not only was she astonished by the glamorous life he lived, but finally she had found somebody who wanted her. For probably the first time in her life, there was a person who welcomed her and saw her as something more than an inconvenience to be endured. A person who saw her as flesh and blood to be loved. That Stanley could offer himself as both role model and father figure – two needs she desperately desired to be satisfied - was a further bonus.

But things were not perfect. Like many people in power, Stanley had some insatiable appetites. He lived for his work; he played hard and had already lumbered his way through three marriages. From one of these, he had two children. They were by then of an age where they would be better placed as siblings than step children to his new wife.

The relationship between children and wife was unstable from the start. Gerri, the daughter and Gary (her brother) resented the twenty-four-year-old; they thought that she was after their father's money and disliked the attention he gave to her. Gerri, who would later become an anchor on local TV, found it particularly hard to get her head around the relationship. Her father was forty and was sleeping with a woman barely older than herself.

But if matters were not perfect for the much in love couple, then they were pretty good. Stanley even adopted Joyce's five-year-old son, making the family complete. Faced with opulence and a virtually unlimited spending capability Joyce set about making up for lost time. The house was decorated and furnished in the most extravagant manner; the very best shops in Miami became her second home. After all, she had to occupy her time while Stanley was working and traveling.

That particular part of Miami, Coconut Grove, is famous for the wealth of its residence but it holds one potentially less salubrious reputation. Among the excellent restaurants are many night clubs. These bright and noisy palaces were home to numerous vices, and attracted what can best be described as a very mixed clientele. The music was loud, the alcohol flowed, the dancing vibrated, and the drugs were openly available.

Joyce lapped it up, as too did Stanley. Life became, for her at least, a cycle of drunkenness and drug induced highs. Night-time became days, and days were for sleeping. It began not to matter too much whether Stanley was with her or not, the girl from the wrong side of the tracks had made an impression and found a place to belong.

But in the early days their relationship was mostly good. They discovered a shared passion for the snow, and trips to ski became a regular winter past-time. Stanley used his vast wealth to build a ranch, a large wooden monolith in the mountains, and the two had a regular weekend retreat. Wolf Run Ranch ran to six hundred acres in the countryside around Steamboat Springs, Colorado. A week in the heat of Miami would be relieved by a couple of days on the slopes. From the outside, their life must have seemed perfect. But, of course, the most beautiful panorama can cover turmoil underneath. That was the position here, especially for Stanley.

He was worried about his young wife's spending, her drinking and her excessive use of cocaine. He did not buy into his children's theory that Joyce was taking him for what she could get, using him as an abundant money tree, but the doubts must have crept in.

Still, he was making money much more quickly than even Joyce could spend, and the property boom showed no signs of abating. What, he decided, Joyce needed was a focus. Something that she could call her own. Maybe if her own self-esteem was built up through a successful venture of her own, her need to do everything in excess might be controlled. He had no doubt that Joyce, as much as he loved her, had been damaged by her childhood, but it was not too late to address this. Not quite. Surely?

So, Stanley bought her a restaurant. Not a small, twenty cover little bistro down a Miami side alley, but a huge, well established and highly regarded palace to food. There, Joyce would act as front of house, greeting diners and making use of her easy going social skills. Dressed and made up to kill, for a while the job provided her with a purpose, but really it was only ever going to be a loosely made stitch sealing the tear in their relationship. Stanley had his work, and his reputation for women. Joyce had her high living.

Spending even more time at nightspots such as the Champagne Bar, she became friendly with Country and Western star Tanya Tucker, who she met at one of the numerous parties she attended. Tanya would tell later of one evening, when the blinds were lifted on Joyce's world, and her unhappiness with life was revealed.

'Bottom line, she was extremely unhappy. Not just sad. It didn't seem like something that was going to go away.'

Joyce believed that Stanley was having an affair, and that his girlfriend was pregnant. He had expressed himself strongly about her spending, and the excesses of her partying and warned that he would divorce her and leave her with nothing. The unlikely liaison was, after a dozen years, falling apart.

The prospect filled Joyce with dread. After more than a decade of the high life, she faced being forced to give it up. Dead end jobs and hand to mouth living beckoned once more. Gone would be the shining Jaguar, the expensive clothes, the trips to every hotspot across the world reached in Stanley's private jet.

And this is where an already intricate story becomes even more complicated. As Miami had expanded and the money flowed in, detritus had been caught in its current. A criminal underworld had grown up, and life for the very rich had its down side. Break ins, and consequent murders, were becoming too common place to be ignored. For Stanley and Joyce, the threat had led them to take steps. Stanley had installed a complex security system at the house and owned his own revolver. They had also bought a dog, a large and aggressive looking Doberman Pinscher they, with gentle understatement, called Mischief. Mischief was fine with people she knew and would greet them with friendliness before drifting back to her own part of the house. But strangers would be put off by the giant black and brown beast lurching towards them, teeth glistening and more than ready to bite. For the all the electronic defences, a dog such as Mischief reached into the gut of human kind and elicited a fear that even hardened criminals would not face down.

But in the early hours of March 7th 1986 Mischief was locked away inside the house, not roaming the grounds as would often be the case. And the electronic security system was turned off. By now, the relationship between Stanley and Joyce had dissolved entirely. They mostly slept apart and he spent much of his time at work or travelling between various interests. Perhaps inevitably, for a man leading construction and real estate development, Stanley dealt with all kinds of people. Politicians, civil leaders and fellow businessmen. Not all of these were from the nicest stock, especially by the mid-eighties, and mixing with the underworld brought its own dangers.

Stanley had been in his room in the mid evening when Joyce heard a noise on the drive. She told Stanley, and he grabbed his revolver and went to investigate. But he found nothing. Why Mischief was not released, nor the security system turned on, following this potential intrusion is a question that would remain forever unanswered.

Rarely now did Joyce sleep with her husband; in fact, she rarely slept at all. While he slept upstairs, she set about clearing some clothes for a sale. It was against the background of this odd arrangement that, in the early hours of the following morning, Joyce heard gunshots.

Reaching her husband's room and she discovered him face down in the bloodied bed. She fled to the phone, dialled 911 and her panicked voice can be heard on the recording.

The operator tells her to calm down, but Joyce cries 'I can't.' She is either a fine actress, or she knew nothing of the planned attack. The police arrived and found that Stanley had been shot four times in the back of the head. He was quite definitely dead. But, it did not look like the kind of robbery against which the Cohens had organised security. A window pane was smashed, but there was nothing taken. It looked as though whoever had broken in had just one purpose in mind, to kill Stanley Cohen.

Police searched the house and grounds and took Joyce downtown for questioning. Although distressed she managed to tell officers that she had heard breaking glass at around 5.30am, or just before. She had headed for the bedroom to get Stanley but saw the back of an invader's head. 'Let's get the f*** out of here,' he shouted and left, according to Joyce's account. Panic stricken, she told how she was rooted to the spot, but finally found the strength to move to Stanley. She told the horror of finding him. Face down. Dead.

Meanwhile, police back at the Coconut Grove mansion were searching for clues. They soon found a revolver, wiped clean of finger prints, thrown away in the grounds. It had not been hidden, just discarded.

The interrogation of Joyce Cohen started gently enough, but soon inconsistencies were beginning to emerge. Investigators suspected that the marriage had been on the rocks. They started to question Joyce about their sex life, which was by then effectively non-existent. Suddenly, she realised that she was not just there to provide information but was a suspect in the murder. She called an attorney and left immediately, returning to her house and pushing the investigating officers out. Even Stanley's body would remain for the eight hours it took to get an official search warrant. But Joyce did not know that the police had discovered a piece of evidence that cast her in a highly suspicious light.

In a bin they had found a used tissue, on which was Joyce's mucus. But also, on the tissue could be traced a touch of gunpowder. It appeared as though she had fired a weapon. More evidence began to emerge. A neighbour reported hearing gun shots at around 3.00 am but it was not until more than two hours later that Joyce had phoned emergency services to tell of the break in. Police were unable to determine Stanley's time of death.

Circumstantial evidence was growing, but the police had nothing concrete that definitively linked her to the crime. Then they got a break. In a completely unrelated investigation, they arrested the head of a gang of home invaders called Frank Zuccarello. While the guilt or otherwise of Joyce Cohen was very much in doubt, irrespective of the gut instinct of Miami's finest, Zuccarello was a crook, plain and simple. He knew that he was facing most of the rest of his life behind bars and was keen to find a way to avoid this.

The murder of Stanley Cohen was a good one to call upon. Unlike some of the larger criminal gangs who might take revenge on he and his family if he revealed their crimes, Joyce lacked the means to do this. Zuccarello started to talk. And talk. He had met Joyce Cohen, he claimed, at one of the nightclubs she loved to attend. He had quickly discovered that her marriage was unhappy, and that divorce was on the cards. Joyce wanted something done about that and was prepared to go to any lengths. Zuccarello teamed up with another couple of hard nosed thugs and Joyce told them all about the house. She warned them of Stanley's gun, promised to lock up the dog and turn off the security system. She gave them a detailed outline of the house, so that they could find their way round. Their task? To kill her husband. Payment for the crime would be made in cocaine – about $150000 worth.

While Zuccarello was keen to tell the story, the other two men involved were less content. Thomas Joslin and Anthony Caracciolo were arrested for other home invasions and police soon put the pressure on to get them charged with second degree murder for the assassination of Stanley. But they would not play ball. Each maintained their innocence. They had never met Joyce Cohen, they claimed, and she had certainly not been a part of any plan to kill her husband, not for either cash or cocaine.

But the pressure increased, and the two knew that they were facing lengthy spells behind bars for the burglaries in which they had taken part. They decided not to contest the murder charges, feeling that to do so would only make their situation even bleaker. That they were threatened with the electric chair if they did not play ball with the police no doubt also played its part. Caracciolo received a forty-year sentence, having been accused of firing the deadly shots, and Joslin was put away for thirty. Despite the sentences, the two continued to state their innocence of the alleged acts.

Some time needs to be taken to consider matters here. Joyce has been questioned but not charged. Suspicions are aroused, but in part at least these have emerged from the sense held by the police that she was a gold digger who was seeing the vein of ore begin to run out. That notion was reinforced by Stanley's children, who had secured an injunction to prevent her getting any hands on the money while the crime was being investigated. In fact, no doubt in part due to Joyce's spending and their lavish lifestyle, while there was money, it was a much smaller figure than might be expected. In the end, Stanley Cohen's estate would realise just $2 million.

The only hard evidence that Joyce was behind the murder was, in fact, not that hard at all. Zuccarello ended up with a substantially reduced sentence for his home invasions. The five years he was given was much less than he might have expected without his deal with the police. He claimed at Joyce's trial that he had witnessed the trigger being pulled on Stanley Cohen and gave a detailed account of meetings with the potentially estranged wife. But he was a crook, under pressure to get a reduced sentence and, claimed the website 'Copblock' in years to come, gently 'persuaded about what might have happened on that fateful night.

Certainly, the trial would see other alleged friends and associates on both sides come out of the woodwork to tell of the unhappy marriage Joyce was experiencing and Stanley was enduring. But there is a considerable difference between being locked in an unhappy marriage, planning a murder and getting it carried out.

Yet when it came to trial the jury were happy to accept the evidence of a confirmed thief and the allegations of others. That trial took a long time to come to fruition. Firstly, police travelled to Chesapeake where Joyce was living in order to arrest her. Life had tumbled out of control for the former socialite. With no access to her former husband's cash, and cast out by his family, she had remarried and was living on a trailer park. Not until two and half years after the murder had taken place did her case actually make it to trial. That lasted six weeks, and the jury found her guilty. Prosecutor John Kastrenakes made a powerful final plea to the twelve men and women charged with deciding on her guilt, and it worked. 'She's a killer, do not feel sorry for her,' he declared. 'She's a cold, calculating murderess who put on a good show for everyone.'

However, while the jury were convinced of her guilt, they were split with regards to the death penalty. With the arbitrators unable to reach a conclusion on this, the judge stepped in and sentenced her to twenty-five years to life for the murder.

Of course, depending on where you stand, the death penalty is either a risky and cruel punishment against which there can be no redress if it turns out that a wrongful conviction is made, or it is a just reward for the most serious of crimes. In Joyce's case, had she faced the ultimate sanction then a serious miscarriage of justice would have been on the cards. In fact, such doubts about her guilt would surface over the following period that any death penalty must almost certainly have been quashed.

In 1993, just four years after her conviction, serious doubts began to emerge as to her guilt. An attorney, Carol Soret Cope, published a book which cast serious doubt on the evidence of the star witness, Frank Zuccarello. It emerged that during his questioning about the murder, he had been subject to three separate lie detector tests and had failed them all. But because the polygraph was not considered as reliable and admissible evidence in Florida courts, the jury had never heard of these failures. It also came out that he had frequently changed his story, sometimes claiming to have been inside the room as Stanley was executed, sometimes on watch outside of it. Next, a local reporter – Gail Bright – discovered previously unrevealed testimony from a leading detective on the case, John Spear. He harboured doubts regarding the involvement of both Caracciolo and Joslin. They too had faced polygraph tests regarding their participation in the crime, and those results were inconclusive. However, Spear's musings suggested that police were confident in Joyce's guilt, and just lacked the evidence to prove their case. The words of Frank Zuccarello provided that confirmation, even if their truthfulness was suspect. A case, it might be argued of justice prevailing over process.

Those suspicions regarding the fabrication of evidence were enhanced following a Miami New Times investigation in 1998. Then, detailed interviews with Joslin and Caracciolo, as well as John Spear, had led them to the conclusion that police might have helped to steer the story along, feeling that truth would be best served in that case.

Of course, the justice system cannot work if police are both investigators and jury; they would be trying their own case. But even more doubt now exists regarding the safety of the conviction. As understanding of forensic evidence has increased over time, one of the key pillars upon which her guilt was pronounced has begun to crack. A criminologist from Dade County, Gopinath Rao, offered an alternative view on the gunpowder infiltrated tissue found discarded in a bin. According to Rao, the small amount of residue could well be evidence of simply being close to a gun being fired, and not specifically firing it herself.

The most recent twist in the tale of Joyce Cohen came in 2013, when her time for parole came up for review. Alan Ross had been her attorney for many years, and he felt that there was no chance that parole would not be granted. The forensic evidence was now open to question; the evidence of Frank Zuccarello had been discredited. Joslin and Caracciolo were continuing to deny ever having met Joyce, let alone carrying our her instructions for murder.

The parole commission chair, Tena Pate, was unconvinced. Turning down the plea for release at the beginning of the following year, she cited Joyce's attempts to cover up the murder. Initially, the commission planned to set a following review date of 2023. But at the last minute, an impassioned appeal from Stanley's children turned the hearing further against their father's widow. In the end, a release date of 2048 was chosen, by which time Joyce, if still alive, will be 97 years old. However, perhaps with a nod to the growing uncertainty around the safety of the original conviction, the commission left themselves with the option of revisiting the case in 2020.

The board listed as a part of the reason for refusing parole the fact that their role was not to examine the evidence once again – that is the job of a re-trial – but to decide whether retribution had been served.

'We're not here to retry the case, she stands convicted of the crime,' said Pate with firmness and resolve.

Alan Ross finds it hard to accept that the testimony of Frank Zuccarello is still allowed to carry any weight. 'You would have to be deaf, dumb, blind and stupid to believe what he had to say,' he argued.

Ross continued with even harder words: 'Are prosecutors turning a blind eye to the obvious perjury? Are police officers turning a blind eye to obvious perjury, even worse, are they supporting it, are they encouraging it? You know, I don't know where the line falls.'

But Joyce Cohen herself is more phlegmatic about her position. Whether she is guilty of murdering her husband through hiring three assassins is something that only she definitively knows. The fact is that the troubled child sought something more from her life, found it and, on her own admission, exploited the position she was in. But she still insists that she did not kill her husband, and what she has been through since that night in 1986 has made her wish that the home invaders had killed her as well as Stanley.

As for the police actions, she has become resigned to the course their investigation followed. 'They had to make it fit. You know, it's like putting this square peg in a round hole. They didn't care what they had to do to get it to fit so that they could get a conviction. Even though I didn't do this, these people know I didn't do this. The prosecutors know that this was not true. The detectives know that this is not true. They know that these people lied, and they used them anyway.'

And now she faces spending the rest of her life behind bars. A fitting punishment for murder? Only if it was a crime she actually committed.

WITCH GIRL : THE TRUE STORY OF MARLENE OLIVE

PAM HAMILTON

Marlene Olive was the instigator in the double murder of her parents in 1975. The killings were referred to in the press as the barbecue murders as the sixteen-year-old Marlene and her twenty-year-old boyfriend disposed of her parent's bodies in a barbecue pit in a state park. Her boyfriend, Chuck Riley would be tried as an adult and sentenced to life imprisonment. Marlene would be tried as a juvenile and released at the age of twenty-one.

EARLY LIFE

The marriage of James and Naomi Olive started out happily enough. The couple had been married for fourteen years and were anxious for a child of their own. They both wanted a girl and found a newborn in Marlene.

Marlene was adopted a day after she was born. James would play the role of the doting father while Naomi would adopt a "very clinical approach to motherhood" according to friends. James had lost his life savings in a failed business project but remained optimistic about the future of his family. He found work with an oil company and was forced to travel abroad. He liked the travel and discovering new places but his wife hated it. She would become an alcoholic shut-in and often accuse James of having affairs which would prove to be non-existent.

"The stage was set for disaster," forensic psychologist Paula Orange said. "Jim Olive was the eternal optimist, always seeing the good in circumstances that looked doomed to failure. And with a schizoid wife in tow, the odds were against him. What would happen in their lives is a classic example of nature versus nurture. Marlene was nurtured by an abusive schizophrenic. How would her life have turned out differently if she had been adopted by a different couple?"

A PARANOID MOTHER

By the time Marlene was five years old, her adopted mother was diagnosed with "schizoid personality with paranoid features." One acquaintance said of their relationship, "she (Naomi) either smothered Marlene or ignored her."

Still, despite the affection she lacked from her mother, she had relatively happy early years as Jim settled his family into the country of Ecuador. But when Marlene was ten years old, she discovered some paperwork in her father's desk.

She found out she had been adopted.

"The story goes that Marlene was playing in her father's den when she discovered the papers," Orange said. "I don't know if I believe that. Marlene was very, very smart. At the age of ten, she probably deduced that the Olives were not her biological parents and began snooping around."

The Olives had no choice to admit the truth when Marlene showed the papers to them. But they did lie to Marlene by telling her that her biological mother had died in a car accident shortly after giving birth. With the truth now in the open, Marlene's relationship with her adopted mother began to deteriorate. The relationship regressed from simply ignoring each other to all-out hatred.

"Marlene became very angry at her parents, particularly her mother," Orange said. "She felt as if she had been bought. She felt alienated from the world at large and this revelation only increased her hatred for her adopted mother. Before she knew of her adoption, Marlene may have held some animosity in reserve as she would have gotten attached to her adopted mother as if she were her biological parent. But now that she knew that there was no blood relation, all gloves were off. Marlene could give into her hatred."

Now, at only ten years of age, Marlene entered a state of confusion. She didn't understand how she could have an adoptive mother which she called "mom" and a biological mother which was her "mom" as well. She began to brood over her "real mom" and wonder about her identity. Ultimately, Marlene would never meet her biological parents (her birth mother was a wealthy Virginia teenager who had a fling with a Scandinavian sailor on leave from his ship).

RETURNING TO THE USA

In 1973, Jim's oil business ventures brought him to the San Francisco Bay Area and the family settled in San Rafael. But their arrival back in the USA was greeted with a decrease in Naomi's mental health. She became even more of a recluse, refusing to leave the home while holding multiple conversations with "voices in her head."

Marlene did not like the Bay Area much at first either. She had spent the majority of her life in Ecuador and was more comfortable speaking Spanish than English. Marlene had been a bit overweight in Ecuador and was forced to attend strict private schools. When she returned to the United States, she was released from the boring school uniforms and realized that she could attract the opposite sex as she began to lose weight.

"It didn't take long for Marlene to go into a rebellion," Orange said. "She had the shock of discovering that she was adopted and then had to deal with the culture shock of moving to the San Francisco Bay Area. She developed ulcers and was given tranquilizers."

Marlene retreated into her own world. She would spend her nights watching horror movies indulging in her obsession for the macabre as well listening to a "glitter" rock performers like David Bowie. She would mimic his dress with platform shoes, tight jeans and she would put sparkle make-up on her face.

As Marlene entered her teenage years, her mother's behavior not only got worse but embarrassed her in front of her peers. Marlene would have friends over the house and Naomi would interrupt their conversation with inappropriate statements.

"Don't pay any attention to her," Marlene would tell her friends. "She's a drunk."

Their arguments then became more hurtful. Naomi would call her adopted daughter a "guttersnipe," a "no good swine", and that she was the daughter of a "whore".

"The mother was schizophrenic," Marlene's attorney Terrence Hallinan recalled. "She used to beat the daughter pretty seriously."

Naomi always kept the curtains closed, as if trying to keep the world out. She spent a lot of time in bed and obsessing over her tropical fish. She was also gaining weight and became jealous of her daughter who was blossoming into a beautiful young woman.

"She started having some pretty serious conflicts with her mother," Orange said. "But, of course, most teenage girls start to have conflicts with their mother during that season of life. Marlene got along fairly well her father but her mother was a whole different kind of strange. On one occasion, her mother took off all her clothes and began dancing around the house, touching her genitals. She would taunt Marlene and say 'this is what your mother was really like. She was a whore. You'll be one too.'"

The labeling of Marlene as a whore became a recurring theme throughout the conflicts between Marlene and her adopted mother. Naomi kept needling Marlene with the accusation that her birth mother was promiscuous and that Marlene would end up the same way.

"Marlene actually began visualizing herself as a prostitute," Orange said. "Because of what her adopted mother said about her biological mother, Marlene actually began to believe she was destined for the same fate and it turned into a self-fulfilling prophecy."

"She (Marlene) was constantly fighting with the mother," Hallinan recalled.

Marlene would fight back, often calling her mother a "bitch" and a "crazy lady who lays around like a pig drinking all day."

The fights would frustrate Marlene to the extent that she would bite on her arms, developing layers of scar tissue over time. These arguments would often end with Marlene locking herself inside the bathroom with Naomi pounding on the door to force her to come out.

Marlene knew that her father adored her. He would arrive home from work and be the peacemaker between the two. He would achieve a stalemate which would never last too long.

By the time Marlene reached high school, her abusive home life would spill over into her schoolwork. In freshman year she was arrested for shoplifting and released to her father after a talking to by the police. She began receiving poor grades and took pills for her "nerves".

She also began dabbling in the occult and started to date a self-professed "warlock". The teenaged boy introduced Marlene to witchcraft and weed as well as sex. Naomi took pleasure in discovering the young Marlene being deflowered in her home.

"Naomi was probably the first mother in history to take a sick pleasure in having her daughter lose her virginity," Orange said. "Naomi took it as a validation of her own prophecy about Marlene, that she would become a hooker."

BOYFRIENDS AS TOOLS

Things didn't last long with Marlene's first boyfriend. Her "warlock" dumped her as he didn't want "anyone clinging to him." Marlene became an emotional wreck and began writing poetry in order to express her thoughts.

"no one stops

to step into my life

and those in it have long ago

fallen asleep.

I have been empty for so long."

With her heart broken and her mother's continuous verbal assaults, Marlene began looking for a way out. A tool that she could wield to eliminate her mother.

She saw that tool in Chuck Riley.

Charles Riley, better known as "Chuck," was an overweight, awkward teenage boy who weighed over 340 pounds by the age of sixteen. His father was a bakery worker and his mother was a nurse's aide. He dropped out of high school in his senior year, finding work as a newspaper and pizza delivery driver.

His life achievements were owning a Hot Rod car and shooting guns but was unpopular in school and in the community until he became a small-time drug dealer. The irony was that in selling marijuana, he became popular and he stuck with that as a career path.

As Riley's confidence grew, he targeted the slim, green-eyed Marlene. She accepted a date with the overweight Riley and the two began dating.

"Chuck Riley was an overweight shy guy with very few friends," Orange said. "So when Marlene not only pays attention to him but agrees to be his girlfriend, he is just head over heels in love and can't believe his luck. He basically becomes her lap dog, he will do anything she says as he doesn't want to lose her."

Riley wanted to impress and keep Marlene so badly that he began making improvements in himself. He began slimming down in weight and changing his wardrobe. He called Marlene "the most beautiful girl in the world" while keeping her happy with free marijuana and adoring words. After dating for only a week, Riley wrote Marlene a note that said:

"I am happy happy happy happy. In love love love love. Do me with me what you will."

Marlene would take Riley up on his words, seeing him as having a "kind of innocence". She did not return his love and affection at first.

"Marlene saw him as a fixer-upper," Orange said. "Maybe even as a useful idiot. She did care what people thought of her so she made him buy better clothes and encouraged him to lose weight. He would lose over sixty pounds in order to be seen as an acceptable boyfriend to Marlene."

With a new boyfriend in tow, the weirdness of Marlene escalated to another level. She identified herself as a "High Priestess of the Satanic Church". Bored during the day and out of school, Marlene would sit on her front lawn, dressed like a witch while "casting spells" on passersby.

Riley was just happy to be along for the ride. Jim Olive liked Riley at first, thinking that the shy and likable guy could be a positive influence on Marlene.

"Jim failed to see the dynamics of Marlene's relationship with Riley," Orange said. "She had all of the power. He thought perhaps that the shy, young fat kid would have some kind of stabilizing influence on Marlene. He could not be more wrong."

"There was no question that Marlene had a lot of influence over him (Riley)," Hallinan recalled. "She could make him do things."

THE LAPDOG

Riley could not believe his good fortune in scoring a young woman with Marlene's looks. Marlene, realizing the power she had in the relationship, began to order Riley to do stuff for her. She had him score free pot and steal things from stores.

Then the thought emerged that she could employ Riley to do something far bigger. She was thinking too small.

She could get him to kill her mother.

"Riley thought that Marlene was playing at first," Orange said. "It isn't like he said 'yeah, sure, I'll go ahead and do that for you. But Marlene kept badgering him and he realized that she was serious."

KILLING MOTHER

"I can't do that," Riley said.

"If you really love me you would do it," Marlene said.

"I can't."

"You can't?" Marlene asked. "You can't save me?"

"Marlene would play up her victimhood with Riley," Orange said. "She activated whatever chivalry buttons the young man had in him. He began to soften on the idea when Marlene began regaling him with the stories of abuse."

Marlene also began to soften up Riley with sex. She made him dress in all black and encouraged him to call her several times a day. When they had sex, they would have "rape" games where he would rip off her clothes. They would then further descend into kink, as Marlene would masturbate with beer bottles, a gun and even the blade of a hunting knife.

"My mother has to go," Marlene said.

"If it has to be done," Riley said. "I would die for you."

The idea of killing Naomi remained just that until Marlene's criminal activities began to escalate. She would steal her mother's credit card and max it out. The couple was then caught shoplifting on a stealing spree that netted them over $6,000 in merchandise. They were caught after being stopped for a traffic violation. The police would find the stolen merchandise as well as drugs and a sawed-off shotgun in Riley's car.

The officers then confiscated Marlene's purse and found a five-inch kitchen knife. She explained the weapon away as something she used "to sharpen colored pencils. I'm an artist."

"There really wasn't much the police could do," Orange said. "Marlene was still a minor and she represented yet another stray youth being sucked in by the drug culture of the 1970s. The police saw her as another delinquent. They would give her a hard time and try to scare her a bit.

Still a juvenile, Marlene was released to the care of her parents. Jim was lenient on her but became adamant on taking away Marlene from her "bad crowd."

"Jim was a little lenient but both parents threatened to send Marlene to juvenile hall," Orange said. "That, of course, would be a death knell to any teenager. They then forbade her from ever seeing Riley ever again and the court followed suit, filing a restraining order against Riley. Jim threatened Riley, telling him that if he ever came around the house again he would kill him. He remained steadfast in his belief that it was Riley that was influencing Marlene and not the other way around."

Naomi herself remained steadfast in wanting to send Marlene to juvenile hall.

In Marlene's eyes, this was her mother's fatal mistake.

It was time to kill her.

ORDERING THE KILL

"Get your gun," Marlene told Riley over the phone. "We've got to kill the bitch today."

Riley and Marlene made a date to kill her parents. But when the day came, Marlene made sure that her father was out of the house. She created a ruse to get her father out of the home, having the always agreeable Jim take her out shopping.

Riley arrived at the Olive residence with a pistol in a paper bag and a claw hammer.

"Riley fueled himself on drugs to calm his nerves," Orange said. "And give himself the guts he didn't have in real life. He didn't want to use the pistol because it would make too much noise and alarm the neighbors. So he planned to crush Naomi's skull in with the hammer."

KILLING TIME

When Riley first arrived he saw the family's green Vega car still in the driveway. Marlene waved Riley off, wanting him to wait until she left the home with her father.

Riley watched from a distance as his girlfriend left with her father.

She left the front door unlocked for him.

Sneaking into the home, Riley would find Naomi lounging on the couch in a drugged out state. Too groggy to put up a fight, she could only hold up her arms in meek resistance as Riley attacked with the claw hammer.

The nineteen-year-old man pounded away with the hammer, sending Naomi's blood splattering across the walls. The claw hammer then lodged in Naomi's forehead and Riley could not wrench the weapon free. He watched as Naomi writhed around on the couch, amazingly still alive.

Panicked, Riley ran to the kitchen and retrieved a steak knife. Determined to finish the job, he stabbed Naomi repeatedly with the knife.

The killing took longer than expected. Riley then panicked when he heard the Vega pull up and Marlene's father head through the front door.

Jim Olive saw his dead wife bleeding on the ground and realized that the assailant could still be in the house. He ran to the kitchen, got a knife, and began searching through the house.

He found Riley hiding behind the sofa.

"I'll kill you!" Jim screamed as he rushed the young man with the knife. Riley still had his pistol inside a paper bag, however, and he fired four shots at his girlfriend's father.

Jim Olive fell to the ground end died.

"Marlene didn't want her father killed," Orange said. "But she wasn't exactly distraught when Riley revealed that he had killed him."

Marlene looked at her two dead parents on the ground and instead focused on a portrait of herself that stood in her parent's bedroom. It was now streaked with her mother's blood.

"Curse that bitch!" Marlene screamed. "Getting her blood all over my picture!"

The two teenaged lovers did not know what to do with the body. Riley sat on the couch frozen, shocked at his own display of violence. Marlene remained calm as she came up with a plan.

First, they would go to visit friends and eat dinner out. Then they went to a drive-in movie before returning home.

They began scrubbing down the house, trying to get rid of all the blood. Marlene and Riley then rolled up the dead bodies in a rug.

"Now what are we going to do?" Riley asked. "Where are we going to put them?"

"We're going to dump them at the China Camp," Marlene said without feeling.

The China Camp was a state park near Marlene's home, an isolated stretch where they could dump the bodies without being seen.

"They soaked the bodies in gasoline," Orange said. "And burned the bodies in an open fire pit. All the while, Marlene was a cool customer, betraying no emotion as the bodies of her adoptive parents burned. She then went and had sex with Riley after they burned the bodies, giving him a reward of sorts for doing her bidding."

The two stood over the fire and watched the bodies burn.

"They should have never been married," Marlene said. "And now they're not."

The next day a hunter had seen the smoke and called in his findings, thinking that a small brush fire was starting.

Firefighters came on the scene but believed that the bones were parts of an animal. They initially believed that someone had killed a deer and burned the body.

Marlene then had a girlfriend come over and told her about killing her parents. The girlfriend then had a threesome with Marlene and Riley. A couple of days later, Marlene had a delayed reaction to the murder of her father, feeling a semblance of guilt as she cursed Riley for killing him. The guilt trip didn't last long as they then took a tour of some nude bars in San Francisco. Sufficiently turned on,

Marlene performed oral sex on Riley then masturbated on top of the gear shift of his car.

"We had to do it," Riley explained to a group of friends who visited the house later. "They wouldn't let me see her."

The two then stole the credit cards off the dead bodies and treated themselves to a shopping spree and fine dining. They also went to a Yes concert.

"Here's the plan," Marlene said. "I figured it out. We're going to wait for the authorities to declare my parents dead. I'll get the life insurance. Then we'll move to Ecuador and live in luxury."

"For all of Marlene's intelligence," Orange said. "She didn't always think things through and let her evil impulses guide her. Riley did as he was told, blindly following the lead of his young paramour."

DISCOVERING THE BODIES

The next week, a business partner of Jim Olive decided to pay a visit to the house of his colleague. He wondered why the usually reliable Olive didn't show up for work or even call in.

Peeking inside the window of the home, he saw what he described as "an ungodly mess." Thinking the house had been robbed, he immediately called the police who came to the house to investigate. The police left an urgent note on the door as Marlene was not home. Confident that she could talk her way out of anything, Marlene came to the station house for questioning.

"Marlene came up with a story that didn't make a lot of sense," Hallinan said.

She told the investigators that her parents were on vacation in Lake Tahoe. What Marlene didn't know was that there was a snowstorm in Tahoe. The police informed her of that then she changed her story, going off on a tangent of having a dream about her father "in a pool of blood."

She told additional stories, none of which made any sense.

"She stated that she had no idea what happened," Police Sergeant Bart Stinson said. "But she said she knew in her mind they were dead."

The detective then had Marlene admitted to Marin General Hospital to be placed on a psychiatric hold.

He then returned to the home, finding it odd that each room had been scrubbed down. The detective did find red specks on the carpet which he determined to be coagulated blood.

Marlene was then discharged from the hospital and declared sane. The assigned detective once again interrogated her and Marlene would change her story multiple times. First, she said that her father had killed her mother then ran away. Then she said her mother had killed her father and ran off. Another story described a burglar killing both parents and another involved Hell's Angels. Then she said her friend Diane Preger helped.

Diane Preger was then questioned by police. She said that Marlene called her over to help clean up her house. Diane recalled that there was blood all over the place.

When they finished, Diane recalled how Marlene and Riley had sex in her mother's bed.

"Marlene just has a way of making you do things," Diane said.

The police decided to talk to Marlene again. This go around, she finally came clean.

She would take the police to the pit in China Camp where they had burned the bodies.

"She tried to justify what happened based on the way she was treated," Hallinan said. "Her relationship with her mother."

Marlene informed the police that her older boyfriend, Chuck Riley, had committed the murders on his own accord. The police arrested Riley and searched his home, taking away incriminating evidence such as three gasoline cans and letters from Marlene.

"I have no guilt feeling at all about my folks," Marlene wrote in one of the letters. "NONE. NEITHER SHOULD YOU. Relax."

"She had manipulated Riley into doing her dirty work," Orange said. "But she was just as guilty as he was in pulling the trigger. When it was time to throw him under the bus, she did so without remorse."

Both were charged with two counts of first-degree murder. Marlene would describe Riley as a "madman" who murdered her parents on his own accord then he held her prisoner for a week as he sexually tortured her.

The double murder shocked the community in Marin County. The press labeled the crime as the "Barbecue Murders" in reference to the two teens burning the Olives in a barbecue pit.

Chuck Riley would be tried as an adult. He was sentenced to the gas chamber but the punishment was later commuted down to a life sentence in 1977.

The courts would be more lenient on Marlene.

"She originally was a juvenile," Hallinan said. "Had she been an adult she would still be in prison."

"It is hard to gauge how premeditated Marlene was in planning out how she would escape," Orange said. "She was clearly in a daze when talking to the cops so the drug use certainly had an effect on the wild and outlandish stories she was given. But one of the most disturbing aspects of the case is how light a sentence Marlene received. It was almost as if she knew she wasn't going to be punished severely so she had no remorse or fear."

Marlene was given a four-year sentence and was sent to the California Youth Authority for confinement and rehabilitation. But just weeks before her release, she escaped.

Marlene somehow made her way all the way to New York.

"Amazingly, she fulfilled the prediction of her mother as she became a prostitute," Orange said. "It was almost as if she were punishing herself for her crime and proving her mother correct. Or another way to look at her behavior is to realize that she thought she was punishing her mother by becoming such an evil person. She would engage in anti-social behavior when her mother was alive to piss her off and now that she was dead she would continue to do so."

"I know she got into some trouble," Hallinan said. "She went to Southern California, she got into some trouble there, there were allegations of prostitution. She got jailed and I kinda lost track of her at that point."

A REUNION

Marlene did visit Riley on one occasion in 1980.

"It was an awkward get-together," Orange said. "Chuck did the majority of the talking. He talked about how badly they screwed up and how perhaps they could help each other in the future. Marlene agreed but totally misunderstood Chuck's premise. Chuck wanted to help improve Marlene's life. She thought he needed drugs, just like old times. They were at different levels so Chuck knew that he would never hear from her again. He knew that he had served his purpose. He literally gave up his life for that girl who now walks the streets."

"I was shy, clumsy, and inexperienced with women prior to Marlene," Riley said during a parole hearing. "I was a virgin. I fell for her completely lock, stock, and barrel into her world. I carried out these acts out of desperation driven by my selfish needs, specifically my need to be with and please Marlene in this regard of the terrible consequences for my action toward Mr. and Mrs. Olive, their families, or the community. Further exacerbating the horridness of our crime, we desecrated their bodies by cremating their remains as part of our ever growing efforts to cover up our terrible crimes. My thinking was confused and distorted. I was in complete denial that I deluded myself into acting as if this murder never happened, all a terrible nightmare to wake up from in the morning. To my core I am truly sorry and deeply ashamed for what I did, decisions I made the murder of the Olive's. I completely and utterly condemn that conduct for which there is no excuse or justification. I take responsibility for these crimes and have taken responsibility for addressing these flaws in my character to change myself to mature."

Marlene would be arrested in New York and returned to the California Youth authority where she was released at age 21. In 1986, however, she was arrested in Los Angeles for running a sizable counterfeiting and forgery ring in the San Fernando Valley. She would be convicted and sent to prison for five years.

Upon her release, she would be convicted again in Los Angeles for making a false finance statement. In 1995, she would be jailed for possessing a forged driver's license.

On February of 2003, Olive would be arrested in Bakersfield on suspicion of passing a fake check, possession of stolen property and counterfeit checks in addition to drug possession.

"Marlene Olive was incorrigible," Orange said. "She lost her good looks but she never lost her ability to manipulate people. She remained a career criminal throughout her life."

ALYSSA BUSTAMANTE

MAGGIE RAWLS

Alyssa Bustamante came from a troubled family. It sparked a rage inside of her that led to one of the most shocking killings in recent memory.

Born to Michelle and Ceaser Bustamante on January 28th, 1994, her parents were cousins by marriage and her mother was only fifteen years old. They moved around the state of California before moving all the way to St. Martins, Missouri when Alyssa was two years old. Michelle wanted to be near her mother, Karen Brooke, who lived in nearby Jefferson City.

Michelle would give birth to a set of twin boys four years after Alyssa and then have another daughter. The teen mother couldn't adequately provide for her young children, however, compiling a record of petty thefts to support a drug habit. Michelle struggled to pay the rent and found herself with three misdemeanor criminal convictions for drunk driving and marijuana possession. Ceaser was even worse, routinely beating Michelle before receiving a ten-year prison sentence for an undisclosed assault charge.

"She (Alyssa) had a very troubled background," Jefferson City reporter Jeff Haldiman said. "A very troubled life. Her mother and father both had issues with drugs and drinking."

At the age of six years old, a hungry Alyssa would walk into her living room and see her mother stretched out on the couch.

Drunk and high.

"Alyssa's mother was not much to write home about," forensic psychologist Paula Orange said. "She would do drugs in from of Alyssa, one time to the point of overdosing in front of her. She would also leave the little girl to fend for herself a lot. She was the type that would say 'there's cereal and milk in the fridge.'"

The sight of her mother down and out on drugs, the absent father, and the daily neglect would prove to be too traumatic for Alyssa.

"Something in her snapped, early on her childhood," Orange said. "There are numerous stories where children are able to overcome horrendous parenting. Alyssa received a lot of help but couldn't do it."

Child protective services would eventually intervene on Alyssa's behalf. They would remove her from her mother's custody and sent to live with her grandmother.

Her grandmother, Karen Brooke, was excited to give Alyssa a second chance at life.

"The grandmother was put in charge taking care of Alyssa and her brothers and her sister by court order due to issues that Alyssa's mother had over the years," Cole County Sheriff Greg White said.

It took some time but Karen would eventually be given legal guardianship over Alyssa and her other siblings in 2002. The children would enjoy living at their grandparents' house which was on a large ranch. There was plenty of room for the children to play both on the ranch lot and in the woods nearby.

The intervention on Alyssa's behalf, however, had come too late.

LIKE MOTHER, LIKE DAUGHTER

As she got older, Alyssa would replicate the life of her mother.

She would pop pills...Tylenol, Thorazine, whatever else she could get her hands on...then lose herself in violent fantasies and suicidal thoughts.

By the age of thirteen, those suicidal ideations would come full bore as she overdosed on some psych meds mixed with some over the counter drugs.

"It was a Labor Day weekend," Haldiman said. "When she had taken an overdose and was found in the bathroom. I think that was one of the bigger warning signs for the grandmother to try and get more help for her."

"She took a bunch of Tylenol and something else," Alyssa's friend, Jennifer Meyer said. "Some sort of pain killer. This was at her grandparent's home. She passed out and her grandma found her and called an ambulance. She had to have her stomach pumped. Then she went to the hospital for awhile and they sent her to a psych ward for awhile. I know she was away from school for like two or three months."

The suicide attempt was an alarming wake-up call for Karen Brook. Alyssa was only thirteen. Teenagers trying to commit suicide certainly wasn't uncommon among teens with troubled backgrounds, but even physicians commented that they never encountered someone as young as Alyssa with her kind of thoughts.

Karen would seek help from as many third parties as she could. She would send Alyssa to several different therapists as well as a psychiatrist who started her on anti-depressants.

A DOUBLE LIFE

Despite her inner turmoil, Alyssa was a stellar student. She never took a day off from school and got nothing less than "B" grades in school. Her teachers recognized her intelligence and she did not appear to have any discipline problems.

"If you had a face to face conversation with her," White said. "You would say to yourself that this is a good choice for a babysitter. She came across very well."

Alyssa, however, had a double life.

She would play the part of the nice high school girl during the day with conservative fashion and make-up. This fooled the teachers and counselors.

But outside of school, this would change.

Alyssa could contort her face into a hard look. She had pale blue eyes which she accented with heavy black eyeliner, drawn into a Kabuki-style triangle, giving her a clownish look. She had light brown hair which sometimes ran down into her eyes. She had plenty of attitude and ran with a Goth crowd.

She fostered this alter-ego on-line, cyber-bullying people for recreation. On her social media sites, she would smear red lipstick which she made to look like vampire blood. She would snarl at the camera and grit her teeth.

SELF-MUTILATION

The angry and bizarre poses on her social media masked a bigger problem. Alyssa hated herself and wanted to cause self-harm. She would take razor blades and make incisions on her arm and wrist.

Psychologists would see this act as a form of self-medication.

Alyssa would carve pentagrams, hearts with a line going through them, and an upside down "Peace" sign. Her largest work was carving the word "HATE" across her belly in large letters.

She would do this cutting as a form of distraction. She would focus on the blade cutting into her skin, the blood coming out...and the pain. She did this as a way to take the focus off her emotional difficulties and make physical pain take center stage.

"The cutting would give her a temporary respite," Orange said. "Alyssa would find herself coming off the high of cutting herself and eventually the bad memories, bad situations, would arise once again in her mind, forcing her to cut herself again. It would become an endless cycle of self-harm."

By the time she was a teenager, Alyssa would amass over three-hundred self-inflicted cuts all over her body. She would also burn herself with matches and bite into her skin.

"There was another side to her," White said. "It was like flipping a switch, going back and forth between the two."

"It was almost like she was living two different lives," Haldiman said. "But inside something was building up. Really building up."

AN ON-LINE PRESENCE OF RED FLAGS

Alyssa would showcase her person on-line as 'badalyssa' among other pseudonyms. In one social media profile, she listed her hobbies as "cutting" and "killing people". These were more than words of bravo from an attention seeking teenager.

Alyssa meant every word.

Her YouTube account was registered under the name Okamikage which was Japanese for "Wolfshadow." She listed her location as "somewhere I don't want to be" and her profile photo showed her with the vampire-style lipstick, pointing a finger at her head like a gun.

Scars from her cutting could be seen on her wrist.

Her YouTube channel (since removed) featured several videos of both her and her brothers trying to replicate stunts they had seen in the show "Jackass". The one revealing video, however, is one that Alyssa titled "Idiots Getting Electrocuted by Electric Fence."

The video starts with Alyssa filming herself touching an electrified fence used to house cattle. She laughs and shudders at the jolt then begins coercing her younger brothers to follow her lead.

"This is where it gets good," Alyssa wrote on the YouTube video clip. "This is where my brothers get hurt."

Her Twitter messages were all dark and more than hinted at an inner rage. She wrote often of "addiction" and "terrors."

"All I want in life is a reason for all his pain," she tweeted as well as "I hate authority."

While in school, she would freak out her friends by asking bizarre questions.

"You ever wonder what it would be like to kill someone?"

But most of her friends would not take her seriously. It seemed as it seemed like idle teenage banter.

"I was at her party," Alyssa's friend Jennifer Meyer said. "And she kind of just took me off to the side randomly and she's like, 'You know, I wonder what it would be like to kill somebody,' because I guess she was mad at one of her friends there, but it just seemed kind of strange. But you wouldn't logically think one of your friends would kill somebody."

Alyssa seemed to be building herself up psychologically to kill someone, The questions and conversations with friends allowing her to psyche herself up for something she wanted to do.

"I'd like to kill her," Alyssa would say, pointing at a random person walking down the hallway at school.

Her words would eventually lead to the deed.

THE MOST INNOCENT

Just leaving a few houses down, nine-year-old Elizabeth Olten would come over to Alyssa's house to play with Alyssa's half-sister.

Elizabeth was a sweet-faced girl with a personality to match. She loved cats, the color pink and was a "girly girl." She had long brown hair and sparkling brown eyes. She was shy but friendly.

"She was somebody special," Peggy Florence said, a friend of the family. "They call her a girlie girl. She would be outside in the snow or in the mud in her frilly little dress."

"Everything that I could tell about Elizabeth," White said. "Was that she was a sweet young lady who did relatively well at school. Her classmates seemed to like her. The teachers had good reports and her mom and family loved her dearly."

"She had frequently gone to the five-year old's (Alyssa's sister) residence," White said. "So it wasn't a huge issue."

Everyone loved Elizabeth.

Everyone except Alyssa as she watched the two girl play act with dolls on the back porch, having a "tea party."

Alyssa eyeballed the young Elizabeth with one thing on her mind. She wanted to kill her.

"I think Alyssa chose Elizabeth predominantly because it was a relatively easy target of opportunity," White said. "And that's a horrid thing."

THE KILLING TIME

In the fall of 2009, Alyssa began planning out how and when she would fulfill her sick fantasy.

She walked into the woods behind her house and began digging.

Plugging in her ear buds while listening to some death metal, she dug and dug, digging two shallow graves.

"She'd been thinking of killing for some time," White said. "And certainly had started to take significant steps toward accomplishing that end."

Alyssa dug the graves out three feet deep. Police would later speculate that she initially wanted to kill her two younger brothers and that the two shallow graves were for them. They pointed to the YouTube video in which she displayed sadistic delight in torturing her brothers by the electric fence. But when an opportunity presented itself in the form of Elizabeth Olten, she took advantage.

"Alyssa didn't care about anyone," Orange said. "Anyone or anything. She was depressed and anti-social. She hated society. She hated people."

Alyssa's diary would confirm her hatred of people and anti-social mindset. On the days leading to the murder, she would write about her cell phone battery dying. There was one long entry where Alyssa would complain about that fact that she could not call anyone to talk about the depression and rage she felt.

"If I don't talk about it," Alyssa wrote. "I bottle it up and when I explode, someone's going to die."

During this time, Karen Brooke would become increasingly worried about Alyssa. A religious woman, Karen realized that all of the counseling, therapy and medication was having no effect on Alyssa. Her granddaughter was still cutting herself and her physician raised her dose of Prozac to forty milligrams a day.

Karen would complain that the high dosage would have an altering effect on Alyssa's behavior. She would come home late when she normally would come straight home after school. She would not come down for the family evening meals, leaving her grandmother to worry about her mental state. Karen would then call Alyssa's doctor and he informed her that the higher dosage of the Prozac would take another month "to level out."

But the Prozac would have no effect on Alyssa. On October 21st, 2009, she would bring her morbid fantasies to life.

AFRAID OF THE DARK

It was starting to get dark. Elizabeth knew she had to get home or else her mother would get mad.

She said her goodbyes to her playmate then started to walk home.

Then she received a call on her cell phone.

It was Alyssa.

"Come back to the house," Alyssa said. "I have a surprise for you."

The girl trekked back to the home and Alyssa led her down the wooded path behind her home. The two walked for quite a ways before Elizabeth started to become tired and scared.

"It's getting dark," Elizabeth complained. "I want to go home."

"Don't you want your surprise?" Alyssa asked.

Elizabeth trusted Alyssa. She was older and seemed nice.

"I don't know."

"Come on, you're going to love it."

"Okay."

Alyssa put her arm around Elizabeth and led her further into the woods. The two walked and walked until the sky grew dark.

Without warning, Alyssa began to attack Elizabeth.

"Alyssa began by trying to cut Elizabeth's throat," White said. "And Elizabeth reached up and grabbed the knife, receiving defensive wounds on the inside of her fingers. Alyssa ends up dropping the knife and begins trying to strangle Elizabeth. According to her statement to us, strangling her until 'the light went out in her eyes.' And then she's down, kneeling across Elizabeth's torso and takes the knife and stabs her eight times. One time sufficiently hard to go through the breastbone, through the top part of the heart into her spine."

"This was her kill fantasy," Orange said. "That is why she tried all three methods of killing. First, she tried slicing Elizabeth's throat. Perhaps that didn't give her the feeling she craved so she began strangling the girl to death. But she needed more. She needed to know what all those fantasies felt like. So then she began stabbing the young girl. Slicing, strangling, and stabbing. She had thought about all three and wanted to know what they all felt like."

The self-harm, the self-mutilation that she practiced on herself was now transferred to harming someone else.

Someone innocent.

Her adrenaline racing, Alyssa dragged Elizabeth's body to one of the shallow graves.

"Alyssa took Elizabeth's body and rolled it to the grave and covered it up," White said. "Stringed some leaves across it and went home. Got cleaned up. Put the knife in the dishwasher."

A HAPPY KILLER

The next morning, Alyssa would write out her thoughts in her journal, expressing the euphoria at what she had done. She described how she had just killed someone, strangled them and slit their throat.

"It was ahmazing," Alyssa would write, going on to say how much she enjoyed it then ending the entry with a snarky "Kay, I gotta go to church now, lol."

Elizabeth's mother had called the police around seven p.m., about forty-five minutes after she was last seen. The community organized quickly.

The search began quickly for the girl. St. Martins, Missouri epitomized small town America. It had just over one thousand people and everyone knew each other. Volunteers began searching the woods behind the neighborhood homes.

Police pinged Elizabeth's cell phone and the GSP led them to the woods but the battery on Elizabeth's cell gave out.

The authorities knew they were close but they could not find Elizabeth.

Alyssa had done a very good job of hiding the body.

"Elizabeth was already dead before we were ever notified," White said. "It was that fast."

Everyone in town thought that an older male predator had snatched up Elizabeth.

"That was the narrative that everyone was used to," Orange said. "Everyone became frantic, talking about any strangers that they may have seen in town. But soon rumors spread that a teenager was involved. Everyone assumed it to be a teenage male."

RETRACING ELIZABETH'S STEPS

Alyssa had not shown up for school the day after Elizabeth's abduction. It was her first unexcused absence.

This raised a red flag to police as they questioned Alyssa. They brought her out back where they asked why she had dug out a grave.

Then they began searching through the house.

Alyssa acted fast. She tried to block what she had written in the diary by scratching out the words.

"We were still able to read some of the words through the writing," White said. "We put a very strong light source behind it and read her original words. At that point, she did confess to it and ultimately take us to the scene of the homicide and to the grave."

Word spread around town that Elizabeth was dead and that Alyssa was the killer.

Everyone involved went into shock. A senseless crime, a murder of an innocent.

Did this really happen?

The brutality of the crime shocked the community. An adult killing a child is rare but it has happened before. No one had ever heard of a fifteen-year-old girl killing a nine-year-old.

"When they announced they had found the body," Haldiman said. "There was an audible hush. They just couldn't believe that, nobody could believe that, number one a child was dead and number two that the person that did it was as young as she was. That just floored so many people. Everybody."

The case became even more tragic as only weeks earlier a panel of psychiatrists determined that Alyssa should be institutionalized for a long term. These clinicians knew that Alyssa was an extreme danger to both herself and other people.

Their warnings went unheeded, however, and Alyssa was returned home.

THE TRIAL

Alyssa would be put to trial and be tried as an adult.

"In this case," White said. "It was clearly, coldly planned, calculated and executed. She executed her neighbor for no reason other than she wanted to see someone die."

While awaiting trial, Alyssa went stir crazy behind bars. She began cutting herself with her own fingernails before placed on suicide watch. Her attorney motioned that she be sent to a psychiatric institution.

Her defense team worked overtime to try and explain Alyssa's murderous act. They recounted the fact that she had been on the anti-depressant Prozac and had been told to increase her dosage a few weeks before murdering the little girl. They told the jury about her upbringing of neglect, suicide attempts and the mental illnesses/drug use of both parents.

But the community-at-large wanted Alyssa's blood. Among the things they wrote were:

"What is a shame is that the Murderer did not die when she tried to commit suicide when she tried to in 2007."

"From what I've heard this girl has had mental problems for some time and has seen counselors or someone in the past."

"Either deport her or send her to the gas chamber. One less sicko wasting our tax dollars."

Prosecutor Mark Richardson would argue for Alyssa to receive life in prison plus an additional seventy-one years.

The years that Elizabeth had lost.

"These sentences are appropriate," Richardson wrote. "And fit what happened to Elizabeth at the hands of a truly evil individual who strangled and stabbed an innocent child simply for the thrill of it."

Alyssa would plead guilty to second-degree murder.

She would take the stand during her trial and betray some signs of humanity, turning to Elizabeth's mother and family.

She expressed how "horribly" she felt for what she had done. Then she suggested that if she could give her own life for Elizabeth's, she would.

The apology fell on deaf ears for both Elizabeth's family and the jury. They felt as if the apology was fake and meaningless.

"I think Alyssa should get out of jail the same day Elizabeth gets out of the grave!", screamed Elizabeth Olten's grandmother.

"She's an evil monster," Elizabeth's mother, Patty Preiss said. "So much has been lost at the hands of this evil monster. Elizabeth was given a death sentence, and we were given a life sentence. I hate her. I hate everything about her. She's not even human."

"Alyssa was pure evil," Orange said. "She told investigators that she killed Elizabeth, that darling little girl, because she wanted to see the light in her eyes go out. If that doesn't make her evil and irredeemable, I don't know what does."

"When a person plans and executes for no other reason that they want to see another person die," White said. "That person is going to re-offend. I think Alyssa is too dangerous to be out of prison.

Alyssa would be sentenced to life in prison but given the possibility of parole. She currently resides in a Missouri women's prison.

Elizabeth would receive the funeral of a beloved princess. Her casket was placed inside a horse-drawn carriage.

All of her friends and family wore her favorite color: pink.

WHEN THE GIRL NEXT DOOR KILLS: THE TRUE STORY OF TYLAR WITT

ERICA FOSTER

"At round one in the morning, the girl snuck the boy into her house. He stabbed her in her sleep, killing her and freeing themselves." This was an excerpt from fourteen year old Tylar Witt's story entitled, "The Killer and his Raven." A story she wrote about her own mother's brutal murder.

Tylar Witt lived in an upscale neighborhood in El Dorado Hills, California with her forty seven year old single mother, Joanne Witt. Joanne worked for the county as an assistant engineer for the Department of Transportation and they lived in an elegant house in a nice gated community. Tylar was a fourteen year old girl who was entering her freshman year at Oak Ridge High School. She was described as a sweet girl when she was growing up. Her mother paid for riding lessons and they liked to stay at home and watch movies and cook, but as Tylar grew up, the behavioral problems began and the fights between the mother and daughter turned into physical altercations. Tylar was turning into a different person, she was becoming a monster.

It all started out as what looked like typical teenage rebellion. Tylar embraced the emo and gothic lifestyle by wearing dark and baggy clothes, she had a love of anime and Japanese cartoons, along with everything violent and connected with death. Tylar met her 'Romeo', nineteen year old Steven Colver, at a coffee shop in the popular shopping center of Town Center Shops, where they both frequented. As Tylar was entering her first year of high school, Steven was beginning his first year of college. He was employed as a Shift Lead at Rubio's Mexican Grill. The duo quickly became inseparable. Tylar looked at the older boy as a god and worshiped everything about him. There wasn't anything she wouldn't do for him. The two were in love.

It was in April of 2009, a few weeks after the two had met, that Tylar approached her mother. She convinced her mother that Steven was gay, so that he would be allowed to rent the extra room in their family home. After much resistance from family and friends, Joanne defended the decision by saying that Steven would be helping her make the mortgage payment, as well as help Tylar with her homework. She was described as very strong-willed by her friends and family and didn't let their opinion of others affect her decision to let Steven move in. Joanne didn't suspect a relationship between Steven and her daughter until one day in May, about a month after Steven had moved in. She entered Steven's room and found Steven and Tylar about to engage in a sexual relationship, or had just finished. She found Tylar naked and hiding in Steven's closet, trying to cover herself up. Joanne was understandably upset and demanded that Steven immediately move out. She called two of her male coworkers to come over and assist her. Joanne informed them that she was kicking Steven out of her house and she didn't want to be alone when she did it in case anything were to happen. The male coworkers helped place all of Steven's belongings on the sidewalk and even threatened Steven before he left.

Vinnie Capatano, one of Joanne's coworkers helping her that day, threatened Steven, "If you make contact with Tylar again, either by phone or in person- I am going to hurt you. And I am going to hurt you East Coast style, not West Coast style." It was an act intended to promote intimidation and scare tactics. Steven looked unshaken, which annoyed Capatano even further. His words didn't seem to bother Steven at all.

Joanne was convinced that Steven had committed a crime by sleeping with her underage daughter and made that clear to Steven before he left. She threatened to go to the police and file statutory rape charges if Steven ever came into contact with her daughter again. He didn't take Joanne's words seriously, or the threats of her coworkers. Steven was later found at least twenty more times after this encounter, sneaking into Joanne's house. All Joanne wanted to do was get her daughter away from this older boy that seemed to influence her bad behavior and irrational decisions. Joanne acted as any other mother in this situation would.

Despite the threats, Steven and Tylar continued their love affair and sexual relationship during the day while Joanne was at work and late at night while Joanne was sleeping. Joanne had expressed concern to a few of her coworkers about her daughter's behavior and the boy that seemed able to control and influence her so greatly. It wasn't long until Joanne found out what was going on behind her back and continued to make good on her promise of going to the police. Steven and Tylar vowed to find a way to stay together, no matter the cost. This is the moment the plotting began between the modern day Romeo and Juliet. This was about a month before Joanne Witt was found dead in her home and arrest warrants were issued for her daughter and her daughter's boyfriend.

Joanne Witt located her daughter's diary and handed it over to the police that were handling the statutory rape complaint. The diary clearly outlined the sexual relationship between Tylar Witt and Steven Colver. It explicitly described numerous sexual positions and encounters that the two had shared. There was no mistaking that there was definitely a sexual relationship happening between Steven and Tylar. The detective called to interview Steven about the allegations and Steven claimed that he was worried about Tylar, but their relationship was platonic. He said he considered Tylar as more of a sister figure, than anything else, and he denied any sexual relationship between the two of them. He also admitted that he was scared of this whole situation and he knew she was only fourteen years old. The relationship between Tylar and her mother was volatile and destructive, to say the least, even before she turned in the diary.

Joanne was a loving and attentive single mother that made her daughter, Tylar, the center of her world. However, an incident that took place when Tylar was five years old, prompted an investigation that removed her only daughter from her home. Tylar was placed into foster care for a brief time before Joanne's parents, Norb and Judi Witt could take her in. Tylar lived with them for 6 months while Joanne attended anger management and parenting classes. The incident occurred when Tylar was just five years old after

Joanne had picked her up from daycare. The young girl was screaming in the backseat which was causing Joanne to lose patience very quickly. Joanne reached back and slapped Tylar. The daycare saw the hand shaped mark on Tylar and immediately reported the abuse to CPS, Child Protective Services.

After Tylar was finally able to go back home to her mother, Joanne was afraid to discipline her like she had before. This gave Tylar the opportunity to do whatever she wanted, knowing she could get away with it. Tylar would threaten to call CPS and report her mother again if she didn't get what she wanted. This created many behavioral problems for Tylar and this manifested itself in the violent relationship between the mother and the daughter. Tylar also reported that her mother was a heavy drinker and she would hit and punch Tylar when she was mad. These allegations were never proven. If the violence and abuse had been as severe as Tylar had made it sound, there would have been noticeable marks and bruises on Tylar. They never found any evidence of the abuse she claimed was taking place at the home. There was constant fighting and arguing. Joanne didn't feel comfortable enough start disciplining her daughter again until the few months before that led up to her murder.

The day that Joanne admitted to taking her daughter's diary into the police, was the same night that Joanne and Tylar got into a horrendous fight at home. Tylar felt betrayed by her mother's actions and began throwing objects at her and fighting with her. Tylar called 911 pretending to be Joanne in an attempt to be taken out of the home. She would have rather been in the Juvenile Detention Center than at home with her mother that night. Joanne got onto the phone with dispatch and when they asked her if she was okay, she responded no. Deputies were on their way to the residence. When the police arrived they saw a cut on Joanne's chin and several bruises. Tylar was taken in that night but was released only hours later, after Joanne refused to press charges against her daughter. Joanne was never required to go to the hospital due to her injuries.

Norbert Witt, Tylar's grandfather, claimed that Steven was a bad influence on his granddaughter, and said that he corrupted her by exposing her to sex and heavy narcotics. Steven was known to engage in illegal narcotics such as marijuana, ecstasy, and cocaine.

Norb and Judi Witt owned a luxury RV and had spent the previous two months traveling around the country. They arrived home only days before they received the call that would turn their world upside down. It was Monday when they received a call from Joanne's boss inquiring if they had any idea as to the whereabouts of their daughter. Joanne had an impeccable work history and never missed work without first calling to let them know. So, when Joanne didn't show up or call that Friday, her coworkers began to worry. They stopped by her home that night and knocked on the door, but there was no answer. Nobody seemed to be home. After Joanne didn't show up to work the following Monday either, they knew something was terribly wrong and called the police to report Joanne as missing. After speaking to Joanne's parents and informing them that they had already contacted the police, they raced over to their daughter's house, which was only a few miles away, so they could check themselves. It is there that they met the police. Norb Witt let them into the house to search. The police informed Joanne's parents that she was found upstairs in her room, and she was deceased. There was no sign of a break in or forced entry, there was nothing missing in the home. But where was Tylar? Better yet, where were Tylar and her older boyfriend?

It didn't take the police long to realize that Tylar and Steven had something to do with the cruel and heinous crime in the Witt house. It was only weeks earlier that Joanne had reported Steven to the police and turned in Tylar's diary. She made her feelings about her mother known in the words scrawled throughout the pages. Tylar even plastered her contempt for her mother across her social media sites. She wasn't shy when it came to sharing her feelings and opinion of her mother.

Tylar and Steven went on like normal the days following the murder. They were living the life they wanted now that Tylar's mother wasn't there to get in the middle of it and stop it. They were seen holding hands and kissing, and had seen some of their friends. It was after a night of smoking marijuana and doing lines of cocaine at Steven's father's house that Steven confessed to murdering Joanne and even showed his friend the bloody knife that he was hiding in the car. This friend was Matthew Wildman. Wildman later testified against Steven and told the court that Steven did indeed show him the knife that was used, and he described how the murder happened, and how Steven stood there when he was finished and watched Joanne die. Steven's father came home unexpectedly so they all left the house, with the murder weapon. The murder weapon was never retrieved after their arrest.

The couple had fled to San Francisco, they no longer cared about the consequences because their plan all along was to commit suicide. If they weren't there, they wouldn't have to face the murder charges. According to their logic, that was the only way that they would be able to stay together, without interference, as well as keep Steven out of jail because of the statutory rape charges. They thought the charges would carry a heavy prison sentence and they didn't want to risk separation due to the diary that Joanne had turned into the police earlier.

While in San Francisco, they rented a hotel room and consumed a bazaar mix of fruit loops, cake and rat poison and each had written out suicide notes. The combination of food mixed with the rat poison didn't work, however, and they were arrested shortly after, before they had a second chance to commit suicide. Alongside the food that was found in the hotel room, police also found marijuana, condoms, Steven's work apron and nametag, and the movie 'Donnie Darko' on DVD. They were found changing clothes behind a dumpster at a shopping mall in the area and were arrested by local police and taken in for questioning regarding Joanne Witt's murder.

Once in custody, Tylar refused to admit that she knew her mother was dead and admitted no fault. She asked for a lawyer and for the detectives to go away. The fateful night her mother was brutally murdered was June 11, 2009. Well into the night, after Joanne had finally fallen asleep, Tylar let Steven into the house. He had acquired a chef's knife from his restaurant job at Rubio's. Tylar had grabbed a knife out of the kitchen in her house, and the two proceeded to go upstairs to the bedroom where Joanne Witt was fast asleep. They had each planned to use the knives they had to kill Joanne....together. Tylar claimed that she could not go into the room with Steven. She fell to her knees and covered her ears, while humming to drown out the sound of her mother being stabbed to death. Steven had taken several practice slashes in the air as a warm up before going into Joanne's room and Tylar said this is what prompted her to stay outside of the room. She chose not to go in with Steven. Joanne was stabbed around twenty times. The fatal wound was a gaping slash in her neck. She struggled with her killer and had put her hands up in defense but the wounds were too severe. A bloody knife outline was left on the bed and a book entitled, "How to Parent your Out-Of-Control Teenager, was ironically nestled in the nightstand next to her bed. Tylar and Steven covered Joanne's body with a blanket, turned the air conditioner down in an attempt to preserve the body, and locked up the house and left. They decided to jump the fence instead of having to put the code in to get out. They didn't want anyone to place them there at the time of the murder.

In a suicide letter that Steven had written to his friends, as a kind of apology for what he had done, he said, "Our souls are tainted...We shall be awaiting our fate in the afterworld."

After the news of Joanne's murder got around, a neighbor spoke up about allegedly speaking to Tylar in the park a few months prior. The neighbor had been walking her daughter to the park and claimed she saw a young girl that looked alone, sad, and even angry. The girl was sitting on the swing set with her face toward the ground. She confronted her and asked what was wrong. She said the girl described a bad home life with her mother, and mentioned that her mother liked to drink and would get violent and hurt her, and they would get into a lot of fights. She said the girl seemed really cold and lost in her replies. When asked what Tylar was going to do to stop it the next time it happened she simply replied, "There isn't going to be a next time. Next time it is going to be either her or me." This statement stuck with the neighbor for a long time after. When she realized that the crime scene was a daughter that killed her mother, she finally spoke to police about the conversation in the park. The neighbor was seen on news footage talking to one of the police on the scene, but requested that her name be left out of the media.

Dan Weiner, Steven's attorney, claimed that it was not Steven that committed the murder, it was Tylar. When describing her relationship with Steven, Tylar said, "I trusted him more than I trusted anyone. And I love him more than anybody or anything. If he told me to jump off a bridge and I asked him why and he said just trust me, I would have done it." This shows just how much influence Steven had over Tylar. When neighbors of Steven's were asked to describe him they had only nice things to say.

"He's always been a nice kid as far as I am concerned. If this is true, it is out of character." –Paul Matloff. He also described Steven as a stand-up kid that never played his music too loudly and was always eager to help his neighbors.

Joan Colver, Steven's mother was quoted by reporters as saying, "He would care about others before himself. Steven is the kind of guy who would drive off a cliff or jump in front of a bullet or run into a burning building....for a friend."

When asked why Weiner felt that Steven was being targeted for performing the actual murder instead of Tylar, he didn't really know why. He backed up his defense and Steven's statement of Tylar being the one to murder Joanne Witt, given her past history compared to Steven's.

"He has never hurt anybody, or tried to hurt anybody or threatened to hurt anybody. As contrasted with Tylar who has a very specific history with her mother, and has literally threatened to kill her, to stab her...the very method by which she was ultimately killed!"

Steven had changed his story and said that Joanne was already dead by the time he arrived at the Witt house that night.

"I think realizing the gravity of the situation after being in jail for a while, it took a while before he was willing to confirm, yeah, that she had done it and how she had done it."

Steven said that Tylar stabbed her own mother to death and then called him over to the house after it was done. That is when he claims to have seen the bloody knife. He said that there was blood dripping everywhere, including some spots on Tylar's pants, but there was no evidence of blood droplets being found anywhere else in the house. It was all confined to Joanne's bedroom where she was murdered. The defense claimed that the police failed to look for blood anywhere else except for the primary focus of the house, which was the bedroom. Therefore, there was no evidence available to back up Steven's story. This new story also came about after Steven had already described to his friends how he stabbed his girlfriend's mother to death in her sleep with a butcher knife. Weiner said that Steven was not homicidal, rather suicidal. They claimed that the plan was for Steven to pick up Tylar and they would run off to San Francisco for a few days and then commit suicide together. There was no talk of murdering Joanne. The defense also mentioned that Steven had a clean record, while Tylar's was filled with a history of violence and running away. Despite the new story, Steven's confession to his friend was more than the prosecution needed. He was convicted based on his own words, just as his mother had predicted earlier.

In prosecutor Lisette Suder's words in her opening statement at trial, she described the couple's actions as "a

19 year old man and a 14 year old girl and their love affair that led to the violent almost to the point of sadistic murder of her mother." Tylar was portrayed as an extremely manipulative and brilliant girl. After lying to the detectives when she was first taken into custody and questioned, she finally decided to tell the truth and later passed a polygraph test proving it. She admitted to conspiring with Steven to kill her mother, but also said that it was Steven that committed the actual murder, while she lay in a fetal position outside of the bedroom. All of the evidence found on the scene corroborated Tylar's account of the events from that night. Tylar, in exchange for her testimony against Steven, received a reduced sentence of fifteen years to life for second degree murder. She would be eligible for parole at the age of twenty nine, instead of thirty nine. They were both sentenced at the El Dorado County Superior Court in Placerville.

Joanne Witt's brother, Michael, shared his feelings before sentencing. He was the one that had been responsible for cleaning up his sister's home after the murder. He said he would never be able to get the images of the crime scene photos out of his head.

"I hope and desire that Mr. Colver experiences the worst possible experiences our wonderful prison system can bestow upon him." The judge had tried several times to stop Matthew's rant.

The trial began with Steven still trying to protect Tylar. He didn't want people to accuse his love, Tylar, of being the mother killer. In the beginning stages of his questioning he would ask investigators if they had spoken with Tylar and he inquired about her well-being. He was sympathetic to her situation and just wanted to help her. He thought they were in it together and their love would keep them connected. It ended with the scorned lovers passing the blame to each other. Steven's defense referred to him as an easily manipulated love-struck teen.

Steven's trial lasted for four weeks but the verdict only took four hours to come back. With Tylar's account of the events, the confession Steven made to his friends, and the DNA found underneath Joanne's fingernails that linked the homicide to a male attacker, it all led Steven to a verdict of guilty, for first degree murder. He was sentenced to life in prison without the possibility of parole.

After sentencing, however, Tylar had an interview in which she admitted, "I still have a really hard time being honest. I panic when I get in trouble and the first thing I want to do is lie to get out of it." This statement could potentially be enough to seek an appeal for Steven Colver at a later date. It showed just how dishonest Tylar could be. So if she were able to say this now, what if everything she said in the trial was a lie, despite the polygraph test.

Tylar's psychologist referred to her as a sociopath. Tylar, in trial, said she had three different personalities that were living inside of her. She had her own personality, an angel named Alex, and a demon she referred to as Toby. She claimed her violent actions that led up to this point were because of the demon. Toby would come in times of intense stress. Tylar also described blackouts that she would experience when she was enraged and tried to use the compassion of her dead mother to sway the jury in her favor.

"My mom was not a vicious person and she didn't hold grudges. Even if something horrible like this would have happened, she would have asked for a just punishment. She wouldn't want to see someone suffer for the rest of their lives for a mistake they made when they were being ignorant and stupid."

The following is a letter that Tylar allegedly wrote to her mother before she was murdered. It was Tylar's plan to run away and commit suicide. It was a good bye letter addressed to Joanne.

"As much as you don't think I love you, I do. Not just because I am your daughter but because you are my best friend. Nothing I have ever said to you in anger was ever true. I would never kill you or hate you....but I can't stand to see you so unhappy, but I am growing up and seeing as you don't love me....the person I have become, I see it only fit I do one last thing to make you happy. You want me gone? I am gone."

In Tylar's testimony she admitted the act of violence toward her mother was not a spontaneous decision. It was a decision Steven and Tylar had made after thoroughly discussing their options.

"I was in shock and then I went into a full blown panic attack, hyperventilating, screaming, and shaking." This was in response to Tylar finding out that her mother had turned her diary over to the police in an attempt to build a case against Steven. They came to their own realization that the only way to save Steven from jail was to murder her mother. There was no way they wouldn't file the charges after all the proof was in the diary. They didn't see another way out.

Steven and Tylar concocted this murder plan, afraid that Steven would be sent to prison for a long time because of the statutory rape charges Joanne had filed against him. They didn't want to risk being separated from each other. They saw the murder and subsequent double suicide as a way of staying together. Just like Romeo and Juliet. What they didn't know was that the statutory rape charges only carried a year worth of prison time, if there was any time at all; it was considered a misdemeanor. Instead of a small charge, with little or no prison time, they exchanged a lifetime of freedom for a lifetime of being locked away due to their irrational nature and horrid actions that were compelled by fear. Neither Tylar, nor Steven were able to determine exactly which one of them came up with the idea of killing Joanne. Tylar had been labeled a liar from the very beginning but all of the evidence they had matched with what Tylar had been saying about that night. Everything fit into place and that's why they believed she was finally telling the truth about Steven.

During Tylar's sentencing the judge addressed her directly, "This was a brutal murder. The court has seen no emotion or even remorse for the loss of your mother...I'm sorry for you Miss Witt, because the person who loved you most and without reservation is gone."

Judi Witt had waited a long time before she would go and visit her granddaughter. When she finally set eyes on Tylar she asked how she could have done such a horrible thing. A look of shock plastered across Tylar's face and she responded, "Do you really think I would have been able to do something like this?" When asked if Judi actually believed her, she responded yes.

Not only did they lose their daughter, Judi and Norb Witt also lost their granddaughter. Judi was able to forgive a little easier than Norb. Norb has since written his granddaughter off for killing his daughter. Her actions were inexcusable. She is not the same little girl that they remembered. They said that the Tylar they knew, wasn't the Tylar that killed Joanne. They choose to remember the little girl that they first visited in the hospital after her birth. Tylar was their third grandchild. They recalled the hospital visit after her birth very fondly. They walked in there with a camera and took many pictures, in awe of their own daughter and their new granddaughter. They choose to remember Tylar as the little girl they had watched grow up, not the monster she had become after killing her own mother, not the girl that constantly defied her own mother and threatened her. Not the girl that wrote in her diary about her dream of finding out her mother had died in a car accident. Tylar had lost her way a long time ago. They choose to only remember the good, but revealed that their family was never going to be the same either. Judi and Norb had come to terms with this.

Norb finally decided to go and see Tylar, after the trial. He had refused to go and see her up until this point. When Norb entered the room, Tylar called him Poppa and embraced him. She began sobbing. Norb held onto her tightly and said, after speaking with her, he could see some kind of remorse for what she had done but he still wasn't in the position of being able to forgive her. "It is hard to forgive someone that helped kill your daughter." Norb and Judi do not visit Tylar in prison, but they do say they write to her very often.

In later interviews Tylar finally began showing small signs of remorse for her mother's brutal ending. At one time Tylar had even considered her mom to be her hero and looked at her as not only a mother figure, but also as a father figure, since she never had a real father. Tylar's personalities were all over the place. She would love her mother one day but threaten to kill her the next.

Steven's mother still holds onto the hope of her son's innocence and the possibility of an appeal. She refuses to believe that the boy she knew would be capable of doing something so unforgivable and so violent to someone else.

The tragic death of Joanne Witt and the story of her daughter and her daughter's boyfriend being the murderers shook the community. A violent history with Joanne and her defiance of any kind of authority figures led Tylar into the arms of someone she felt could protect her. The two scorned lovers had a premeditated and thought out plan to kill the object of their resistance. According to their teenage logic, getting rid of Joanne and committing suicide was the only way they could ever be together. Even the most thought out plans tend to backfire, however, and they were very much alive while Joanne was gone. They traded a life of freedom with some restrictions, for a life spent behind bars. They miscalculated the situation and now live to regret it, day after day, year after year.

WHEN GIRLS NEXT DOOR KILL : THE TRUE STORY OF MELINDA LOVELESS

IRIS OWEN

"Melinda Loveless is the closest thing you will ever look at and know what the devil is. Her eyes are empty. There's nothing inside of her." - Jacqueline Vaught, mother of Shanda Sharer.

BIRTH OF A MONSTER

Melinda Loveless was born on October 28th, 1975 in New Albany, Indiana to Marjorie and Larry Loveless. Melinda would be the youngest of three daughters born to the couple. Her father, Larry, would be a celebrated Vietnam veteran who would be given a hero's welcome in his return home. Behind closed doors, however, Larry was a certified nut who abused his wife and children.

After returning home from military service, Larry would work for the Southern Railroad before becoming a probationary officer with the New Albany Police Department. He would be fired after only eight months on the job after he and his partner would be convicted of assaulting an African-American man.

Larry would justify the assault as he believed that the man slept with his wife.

The incident would be a bit of a head-scratcher as Larry had fantasies of being a cuckold. He would bring his co-workers home to have sex with his wife so he could watch. He would also introduce his wife to a swingers lifestyle.

Larry was a hedonist. He indulged in whatever pleasurable whim his mind could dream up. This also meant spending exorbitant amounts of money. He would buy motorcycles, cars, guns, and other gadgetry. It all became too much as the couple would file for bankruptcy in 1980.

Seeking to turn his family's destiny around, Larry decided they needed religion. He would gather up Melinda and her sisters to attend the Graceland Baptist Church. Both Larry and Margie vowed to stop drinking and put an end to their swinging lifestyles. Larry would soon become a recurring speaker in the church, taking the podium and talking about how Christ had changed his life.

Bad judgment would remain at the forefront of their lives, however. They would let Melinda go with an older man to a hotel room by herself as he claimed he needed to perform an exorcism on her. Larry would become one of the resident family counselors in the church. He would talk to a troubled husband and wife privately and invariably make a pass at the women. He tried to rape one of them and was then excommunicated from the church.

After that incident, Larry decided to turn his back on religion and anything that resembled taking the high road in life. He and his wife would then resume their partying ways with booze and swinging.

CRIMINAL PERVERSIONS

Larry would state that he and his wife had an open relationship. They would enter bars together in Louisville and Larry would pretend to be in the medical field, acting like a big shot doctor or dentist. He would introduce Marjorie as his girlfriend but proceeded to hit on whichever bar girl caught his eye. He would also allow some of his friends from work to have sex with Marjorie but she found his co-workers to be repulsive.

They would have sex orgies with other couples. On one occasion, Margie tried to commit suicide afterward as the experience was so degrading.

Undaunted, Larry would direct a gang rape of Margie and she again tried to kill herself by drowning. She would deny Larry sex for over a month until one night he became so frustrated that he raped her in front of Melinda and her sisters.

Yet she remained with him.

Around 1986, the couple were again in a seedy Louisville bar with Larry chatting up two women. He wanted to take the women home but Margie would not let him. Enraged, Larry would beat his wife up so bad that she was sent to the hospital. He would later be convicted of battery.

By 1988, Larry began working for the United States Postal Service but quit after three months. He loafed around on the job and would often bring undelivered mail back to his home to burn. With little money coming in, visiting extended family would often complain that the Loveless daughters looked undernourished.

INCEST

The rumors about Larry sexually abusing his daughters remain uncorroborated. There were court testimonies that he had fondled Melinda's older sister Michelle when he was a baby. There were also allegations that he molested his wife's thirteen-year-old sister as well as Melinda's cousin for several years.

Melinda's cousin would testify in court that Larry tied all three sisters up in the garage and raped them on by one. Both of Melinda's sisters have said that he molested them but Melinda herself would not admit that it ever happened to her.

She would, however, sleep in bed with him until she was fourteen when he finally left the family.

What is certain was that Larry had a traumatizing effect on all of his daughters. On one occasion, he fired a gun in Michelle's direction when she was only seven, missing intentionally but trying to scare her. He would also take the girls' underwear from the laundry and smell it in front of family members, trying to humiliate them.

Margie would then catch Larry "spying" on a then fifteen-year-old Melinda and her friend. Enraged, she grabbed a knife and began slicing at him. He was able to wrest the knife away from her but had to go to the emergency room for injuries suffered during her attack.

"Margie had an inability to cope," forensic psychologist Paula Orange said. "She tried religion, counseling, hedonism. It all didn't work. Larry was a pervert with a personality disorder. He would run right over Margie and do whatever the hell he wanted. This traumatized Melinda obviously. Her father was abusing her and others while her mother's only response was to try and kill herself."

Margie would try and kill herself one last time but her daughters were able to intervene. Larry would then divorce Margie, wanting to start a new life. He left behind all of his daughters, remarried and moved to Florida.

Melinda took her father's absence the hardest. Larry would humor her for a little while, writing her letters.

Soon the letters stopped and their relationship deteriorated to having no contact.

"The divorce would have a great impact on Melinda," Orange said. "Her home life was horrid, obviously. She had no guidance other than her mother's Christian fundamentalism which would be offset by the way she lived her life. Melinda was raised by spiritual schizophrenics if you will. What she ultimately did was her choice but she did not have any sort of checks and balances in place when she was a child."

Melinda's father, Larry, would be arrested in February of 1993 after open court testimony revealed that he had abused his wife, daughters and their cousin. Because most of the crimes took place between the years of 1968 to 1977, all but one of Larry's charges would be dropped to the statute of limitations in Indiana. He would plead guilty to one count of sexual battery then be released in June of 1995.

He then tried suing the Floyd County Jail system for $39 million dollars. Among his primary complaints during in incarceration was that he was now allowed to sleep during the day or read the newspaper.

His lawsuit was unsuccessful.

THE DOWNWARD SPIRAL

Melinda's behavior became increasingly erratic after her father's rejection. She would get into fights at school and exhibit signs of clinical depression. At the age of fourteen, she entered into a lesbian relationship with a classmate named Amanda Heavrin. Her mother expressed anger at Melinda's sexual orientation but would eventually accept it. Melinda's relationship with Amanda, however, would eventually deteriorate.

The two were not dating when Amanda would become enamored with a younger girl named Shanda Sharer. Melinda would see the two talking outside a school dance and go into a jealous rage.

What she didn't know was that the fifteen-year-old Amanda was smitten with the twelve-year-old Shanda.

Amanda, both looked and dressed like a young boy. She cultivated a "boy band" look and had a sweet disposition that put Shanda's guard down. Shanda was a lonely wallflower at the school. She had recently transferred in and did not have any friends yet. Amanda took advantage of the situation, sending the young girl love notes, flowers and calling her one the phone.

Shanda liked boys but Amanda remained persistent. She knew that Shanda was flattered by the attention and grateful for her company. The new school was a lonely place for the young twelve-year-old.

Their friendship turned into a romance.

And Melinda Loveless could not have that. Amanda was hers and hers alone.

SHANDA SHARER

Shanda and Amanda would spend an increased amount of time together as the school session wore on. When they weren't together, they were writing each other notes or talking on the phone. Shanda's mother, however, caught wind of the relationship and did not approve. She thought Amanda was too old to hang out with Shanda, who was only twelve. The fact that Amanda was a lesbian only raised her eyebrows further.

Shanda was born in Pineville, Kentucky on June 6th, 1979 to Stephen Sharer and Jacqueline Vaught. Her parents would divorce early in her childhood and Shanda would move with her mother to Louisville when she remarried. Shanda would excel in school, receiving good grades while participating in cheerleading, volleyball, and softball. Her mother would divorce again when she was twelve and the family would move to New Albany, Indiana. She would then transfer into a Catholic school after her parents worried about her relationship with Amanda Heavrin. While at Our Lady of Perpetual Help, Shanda played on the basketball team and proceeded to get her life back in order.

"I met her in junior high," Amanda Heavrin recalled. "We became very, very close. We became really good friends."

But Amanda's feelings toward Shanda would only enrage Melinda. Shanda was the passive recipient of Amanda's attention but Melinda didn't see it that way. She would send Shanda notes, one of which read:

Amanda and I are going together and she loves me and I love her and she only wants to be friends with you. You need to accept that! You need to find you a boyfriend because Amanda is mine.

"Shanda would go up to the teacher's desk and Amanda would be staring at her," Melinda said. "I'd see her and Amanda laughing and passing notes and I'd get mad."

The jealousy would eventually come to a head at the school dance. Melinda saw Shanda talking with Amanda outside and immediately confronted her young rival.

"She tried to beat Shanda up," Amanda said. "I got between them and told Shanda to run."

Melinda would be distraught afterward. She began a letter writing campaign to Amanda.

"I want Shanda dead," Melinda wrote.

"I didn't think she was capable of murder," Amanda said. "I thought maybe she'd just try to scare her. Beat her up or something. That's the Melinda I knew. I didn't know her as being a violent person."

TEEN GIRL KILL SQUAD

Melinda wanted Shanda dead.

With murder on her mind, Melinda would enlist the aid of three of her friends. Laurie Tackett, Hope Rippey and Toni Lawrence. Three teenage girls who all had similar, troubled backgrounds. The amount of psychiatric medications prescribed to each of the four teens would be enough to supply a psych ward for a year...and together they would make for an uncontrollable, unpredictable mob.

Together, they would drive over to Shanda's house and listen as Melinda told them of her plan.

But who were these girls that were so easily persuaded to murder?

First, there was Laurie Tackett, born in Madison, Indiana in 1974. She came from a religious family as her mother was a fundamentalist Pentecostal Christian. Taking on extremist views, her mother attempted to strangle Laurie when she found out that she was changing into jeans at school. Her mother also came to Hope Rippey's house unannounced after finding out that Hope's father had given the girl's a Ouija board. She then demanded that the board be set on fire and that Hope's house should be exorcised.

Laurie's father was a convicted felon who worked in a factory. She would later claim she was molested at the ages of five and twelve. Child protective services became involved and would come to Laurie's house unannounced to ensure that she was not being abused.

Laurie would rebel against her parents and would take a profound interest in the occult. She would entertain her friends as she would pretend she was "Deanna the Vampire", acting as if she were possessed.

She would enter into a lesbian relationship at the age of seventeen and her girlfriend would introduce her to self-harm. Her mother would discover her self-mutilating scars and check her into a mental hospital. Laurie would be prescribed anti-depressants upon her release but would slice her wrists again only days later. She would then be diagnosed with borderline personality disorder after a second stint in the psychiatric ward.

Having no goals or concern about the future, Laurie would drop out of high school

An elementary school friend of Laurie, Hope was born in Madison in 1976. Her parents would divorce when she was eight and she would move with her mother and siblings to Quincy, Michigan. Her parents would get back together, however, and the family would return to Madison in 1987. She had grown up with both Laurie and Toni Lawrence and was happy to be reunited with them. Her parents were leery of Laurie, however, and wanted Hope to steer clear from her. Like Laurie, however, Hope was troubled and begin to self-harm at the age of fourteen.

Toni Lawrence rounded out Melinda's trio of killers. She was born in Madison in February of 1976. She would be molested by a relative at age nine and later raped by a teenage boy at age fourteen. The boy would not be charged with the crime, instead, the police only issued a restraining order. Toni would go into therapy after the assault but refused further treatment after a couple of sessions. She would later begin to self-harm as well as sleep around with other boys, getting a reputation as a "whore". She would try to commit suicide in eighth grade.

The stage was set as Melinda had assembled a group of young girls that were just as damaged as she was. Girls that were ticking time bombs. Alone they would have done nothing violent. But together? Together they would be capable of the most horrific crime imaginable.

"Everything that horrible that happened to each of those girls," Shanda Sharer's mother, Jacqueline Vaught said. "Everything that happened to them, they took it out on my child. I think that's what they were doing, I think they just all exploded that night."

The four teenagers drove around the Indiana back roads as Melinda detailed her plan. Laurie was in the driver seat as she was the only one old enough to drive. All piled in, Melinda would tell her acolytes of her plan to scare a girl named Shanda. She pulled out a kitchen knife from her jacket and showed it to the girls.

She's a copycat," Melinda said. "I want to scare her for stealing my girlfriend."

"I'm tired of hearing you just talk about hurting her," Laurie said. "If you really want to hurt her you should go ahead and really do it."

Melinda took the challenge. She needed a volunteer to lure Shanda out of the home. She knew that Shanda's parents were no longer allowing her to see Amanda anymore. But if they could use Amanda as bait, they could lure her out.

Melinda knew Shanda's address but the girls got lost a few times and stopped to ask for directions.

Finally arriving at the home, Melinda sent Hope Rippey to the door.

Jacqueline Vaught came to the door and saw Hope in front of her. She had never seen the teen before but didn't think anything wrong when Hope politely asked if Shanda was home.

"Shanda had never been anywhere where we didn't know where she was or who she was with," Vaught said. "Shanda was not allowed to go to anybody's house where I didn't call the parents that I didn't go there. I was very, very protective."

She called Shanda down and left the teen girls alone.

"Your friend Amanda is upset and really needs to talk with you," Hope said.

"Why?" Shanda whispered, looking back to make sure her mother wasn't listening. She was no longer allowed to have anything to do with Amanda.

"She's waiting for you at the Witches Castle."

Shanda knew that Hope was referring to an old, stone house, located on an isolated hill next to the Ohio River. It was a creepy but teens like to hang out there.

"I'm having nothing more to do with Amanda."

"Have a heart," Hope said. "You must care about her, couldn't you be there for her just one last time?"

"Why did Amanda send you instead of coming herself?"

"Amanda knew she couldn't come to your house."

"I can't go now," Shanda said, looking behind herself again. "My parents are up. I'll sneak out around midnight if you want to come back hen."

Hope agreed and returned the car without Shanda.

Melinda immediately confronted Hope on why she didn't have Shanda with her. Hope explained that Shanda agreed that if they came back at midnight, she'd be willing to come with them.

The teens then head out to a nearby punk rock concert. Both Toni and Hope get bored and have sex with two boys they've just met to pass the time.

Midnight rolled back around and the girls returned to Shanda's home.

"I can't wait to kill Shanda," Melinda said. "I'd like to fuck her."

Melinda then hid in the back seat. The other girls covered with a jacket and trash from inside the car.

Hope then went and got Shanda.

"They were not mean looking, dirty child molesters," Shanda's mother, Jacqueline Vaught said. They were two children that looked like her. They said just walk twenty-five feet and talk to her. And that's what she did."

Shanda squeezed into the front seat, sitting in between Laurie and Toni. The girls pretended to like Shanda at first but soon she began feeling uncomfortable.

"The Witches Castle is a short drive away," Laurie said. "You know the legend? That house had once been owned by nine witches who had controlled the town and the townspeople had burnt the house to get rid of the witches."

"So what's up with you and Amanda?" Hope asked, turning to Shanda.

"We'd been going out for quite awhile," Shanda said. "I really cared about her."

"I see."

"What's wrong with Amanda?" Shanda asked. "Why does she have to see me so badly?"

"Surprise!" Melinda screamed, jumping out from the backseat. She grabbed Shanda's hair, pulled her head back and put the knife to the young girl's throat.

"Please don't hurt me," Shanda said.

The girls all laughed.

Laurie stepped on the gas...

CRUEL AND SADISTIC

"Bitch," Melinda hissed as she pressed the knife down on Shanda's throat. "Don't move, don't make a sound."

They arrived at the Witches Castle, parked and pulled Shanda inside. Melinda tied up Shanda's hands with a rope. Hope waved the knife in front of Shanda's face, taunting her. Laurie took along an old t-shirt and set it on fire.

"You see that?" Laurie held up the burning shirt before the crying Shanda. "That's what you're going to look like before the night is over!"

Melinda then ripped off Shanda's necklace and bracelets. She handed them to Toni and they took turns admiring the items. Hope ripped off the Mickey Mouse Musical watch from Shanda's wrist and put it in her pocket.

Several cars passed before the castle and then the girls went quiet, waiting for the coast to clear. Not satisfied that they would have total privacy, the girls dragged Shanda back to the car and stuffed her in the back seat, covering her with a blanket.

Laurie made a pit stop at a gas station while Melinda stood guard over Shanda. Hope went inside to pay for the gas while Toni makes a phone call.

She does not tell the person she is calling about the kidnapping or ask for help.

The girls then go back to their hometown of Madison, Indiana, an hour away.

Once there, they drove a few miles past Laurie's home and pull off into a seldom used logging road. Laurie stops the car and they all get out. Hope and Toni complain about the cold and wait inside the vehicle.

Melinda then hauled out Shanda from the back seat. The girl resisted until Laurie came to help and they muscle her out of the vehicle, throwing her to the ground.

"Take your clothes off, bitch," Melinda screamed.

Crying, Shanda complied with the request. Hope and Toni watch from the car window.

Melinda then took Shanda's clothes and threw them into the back seat. "I want them as souvenirs.

Playing along, Hope put on Shanda's polka dot bra. Toni turned on the radio.

"Shanda had hugged me," Laurie said in a December 1992 interview. "She asked me not to let Melinda do it. She was crying. There wasn't anything I could do."

Laura instead held Shanda's hands behind her back. Melinda then began punching the little girl.

"Please let me go," Shanda screamed. "I'll stay away from Amanda."

"Shut up!" Melinda punched Shanda hard in the stomach. She followed this up by pulling her by the hair as she fell to the ground. Shanda was prone and Michelle repeatedly kneed her in the mouth

Shanda winced and yelped in pain.

Her adrenaline and nerve increasing, Melinda took out her knife and tried to cut Shanda's throat. The blade is too dull, however.

"Get over here, Hope!" Melinda commanded.

Hope obeyed and Melinda ordered her to help hold Shanda down. Melinda then tried to use her foot to pierce the knife through Shanda's throat.

The girls then took turns stabbing Shanda in the chest.

The knife was still too dull.

"We need to just strangle her," Laura said, taking the rope and wrapping around her neck.

"Please don't kill me," Shanda pleaded.

Melinda just laughed. She sat on her Shanda's legs as Laura straddled her chest, tightening the rope.

Shanda would pass out and the girls thought she died. They picked up her body and tossed her in the trunk of the car.

POINT OF NO RETURN

The girls would arrive at Laura's home, triumphant. They would go upstairs to Laura's bedroom and drink soda. Laura, the occult aficionado, would take out her "runes stones" and perform a "future reading" for the girls.

"Our futures look good," Laurie said until they heard her dog barking outside. The teens rushed to the window and listened. They could hear Shanda screaming from the trunk of the car.

Laura went to the kitchen and got a paring knife. She hurried outside, opened the trunk and began stabbing Shanda repeatedly. The girl quieted down and Laurie closed the trunk again.

Laurie returned to her bedroom, covered in blood. She washed herself up and then addressed the kill squad with a renewed need for cruelty.

"We have to go for a ride," Laurie said.

"I'm tired," Toni said.

"Me too," Hope agreed.

Melinda and Laurie dismissed the girls and went for a drive by themselves. They headed back to the isolated road, parked and then went to check of Shanda had died yet.

The little girl sat up. Her eyes rolled in the back of her head. She tried to speak but was only to say one word.

"Mommy."

AN ENDLESS NIGHT OF TORTURE

Laurie picked up a tire iron from the trunk and bashed Shanda across the head. She closed the trunk again and they drove along the back roads. The mood turned somber and silent until they once again head Shanda choking in the back trunk.

Laura stopped and got again, opening the trunk and bashing Shanda in the head the tire iron once more. This time, a chunk of flesh from Shanda's temple went flying into the night air.

Laurie came back to the car, blood splattered across her arms.

"She looked as though she was painted red," Laurie laughed, waving the bloody tire iron and under Melinda's nose who smelled it with glee.

Melinda and Laurie then go back to Laurie's home. The woke up Toni and Hope, laughing and filling them in on how much further they tortured Shanda. The foursome discussed what they should do with the body until Laurie's mother woke up.

She berated her daughter for being out so late then yelled at her even more for having her friends spend the night without asking.

After her mother's lecture ended, Laurie led the girls to the back of her house.

ONE LAST ACT OF EVIL

"There's a burn pile out here ," Laura said, skipping through the woods beyond her back yard. They would find the burn pile but it would be covered in frost.

"That won't work," Laura said. "We're going to need some gasoline."

The girls went back to the car and opened the trunk, needing another look at their victim.

Toni refused to look at the tortured body of Shanda, shocked by the amount of blood covering the girl.

"Start the car and rev the engine if she starts screaming," Laurie said.

Hope grabbed a bottle of Windex in the trunk and began spraying Shanda's body.

"You're not looking so hot are you?" Hope taunted.

Shanda was semi-conscious. She sat up, her naked body covered in dried blood.

"Laurie!" Laurie's mother called out.

"Shit," Laurie slammed the trunk lid on Shanda's head and went to find out what her mother wanted.

After a few minutes, Laurie returned and the girls drove to a gas station. Laurie ordered Toni to buy a two liter Pepsi bottle from inside. She came back and Laurie emptied the bottle into the dirt then filled it with gasoline.

"We could get rid of her out by Lemon Road," Hope offered.

Laurie followed Hope's directions, driving onto the old country logging road. Toni would remain in the car as the three other girls pulled Shanda out from the vehicle.

Hope would pour the Pepsi bottle filled with gas over Shanda. Laura lit a match and tossed it on the body.

The fire blew high. The girls giggled and ran back to the car, speeding away.

"Wait," Melinda said. "Turn the car back around."

"The way it was told to me," retired detective Steve Henry said. "Was that they drove away and turned around and came back past the body thinking that she would be burned completely up and there would be no trace of her and she was still there so Melinda set her on fire again."

Laurie complied, doubling back and stopping in front of the burning body. They watched for a few minutes until Melinda stepped out of the vehicle with the Pepsi bottle.

She looked down on Shanda, her body in a fetal position. Tongue lolling in and out of her mouth as she convulsed in pain.

Melinda poured the remainder of the gas on Shanda and tossed another match on the little girl.

The teens then drove off and ate breakfast at a McDonald's.

"What does this remind you of?" Laurie asked as she held up a piece of sausage.

"Shanda's body," Melinda laughed. "Burned to a crisp."

Shanda was not dead yet, however. Soot was later found in her airways which meant that she was burning in the fumes around her. She was conscious while they set her on fire.

"They didn't know how to tell me how she died," Shonda's mother, Jacqueline Vaught said. "And I saw it on television. That she'd been burned alive. I didn't know that."

Melinda would then call her ex-girlfriend, Amanda Heavrin and confess to the crime.

"She told me everything that happened," Amanda recalled. "I thought it was a joke. Because I just cannot fathom that four little girls would do this to another human being. This is stuff you wouldn't even do to an animal."

She thought that if she removed the competition that she could have Amanda.

CONFESSION AND TRIAL

Toni Lawrence would be the girl to come forward and confess. She came home hysterical, telling her parents what happened. They took her down to the police station and she told detectives what happened.

All four teenagers would be charged as adults. This forced them to accept plea bargains as they wanted to avoid the death penalty.

The defense played on the fact that all four girls were victims of physical and/or sexual abuse in their childhood. Hope, Toni, and Laurie had histories of self-harming behavior. Laurie was clinically diagnosed with a borderline personality disorder and had both visual and auditory hallucinations.

Toni would cooperate in exchange for a lesser sentence. She was allowed to plead guilty to one count of criminal confinement which got her a maximum sentence of twenty years. Hope would be sentenced to sixty years with ten years suspended for mitigating circumstances plus ten years of medium-supervision probation. She would continue to appeal and the judge would reduce the sentence to thirty-five years. Both Laurie and Melinda wold be sentenced to sixty years and sent to the Indiana Women's Prison in Indianapolis.

Melinda's attorney would appeal for her release in October of 2007. He would argue that Melinda had been "profoundly retarded" by the abuse she suffered during childhood. He further argued hat she had not been competently represented during her initial sentencing. He also played the "age card", as Melinda was only sixteen years old when she entered the plea agreement with the state of Indiana and needed consent from a parent or guardian.

The appeal for her release was denied but the sentencing was reduced down to make her eligible for parole in fifteen years. It is becoming apparent that Melinda and Laurie could be released from prison as early as 2022.

Toni would be released from jail in December of 2000 after serving nine years. She would remain on parole until 2002. Hope was released

from the Indiana Women's Prison on April 28, 2006, serving for
fourteen years.

"None of these girls were born murderers," Vaught said. "They
weren't born to murder children. They weren't born to be in prison.
This what we do as parents. We mold our children into what they are."

Shanda's father, Stephen, would die at the age of 53 due to alcoholism.
Stephen had become depressed over the death of his daughter and
subsequently "drank himself to death" over the years.

"Steve could not have been a prouder father," Vaught said. "Shanda
was his life. From the day that she died he did everything he could to
kill himself beside put a gun to his head. And finally he drank himself
to death and he died at fifty-three."

"Melinda has cheated me out of being with my daughter during
this life. It is my wish for you (Melinda) that you live your life with
memories of her screams and sign of her burned and mutilated body. I
hope and pray you remember these words for the rest of your life: May
you rot in hell."

WHEN GIRLS NEXT DOOR KILL : THE TRUE STORY OF CINDY COLLIER & SHIRLEY WOLF

IRIS OWEN

"Today, Cindy and I ran away and killed an old lady. It was lots of fun" -
Shirley Wolf's journal, June 14th, 1983.

Shirley Wolf and Cindy Collier met in a juvenile detention center and had known each other for only a few hours when they decided to escape and randomly kill a stranger.

They would go to a senior condominium center in Auburn, California where they would seek an elderly victim.

They would find one in the eighty-five-year-old Anna Brackett. They entered her home under the ruse that they needed to use the phone to call their parents.

The girls would brutally murder the elderly woman in a crime so shocking that deputy sheriffs were initially in denial that two young girls would commit such a crime.

But how did they get to the point mentally where they could commit such a horrid act? This is the story of how they got there.

EARLY LIFE

Cindy Collier wasn't the nice girl next door. Her entire body language spoke of rage and hostility. By the age of twelve, she was a regular at the juvenile hall where she would routinely assaulting staff and inmate alike.

Incorrigible, she had been arrested for burglary, theft and drug possession.

Because of her age, Cindy was often spared jail time and was sentenced to community service. She would most often be sent to pick up litter on highways but the punishment wasn't enough to deter her from a life of crime.

"She was a smart ass towards everyone," former classmate Mike Fluty said.

No one was spared her rage. At fourteen years old, she had no problem harassing adults as well, randomly accosting people on the street.

"What are you looking at?" she asked a woman walking by as she smoked a cigarette. "You think you're better than me?"

She would then raise her fist to the woman and force her to run away. "Oooh!" Cindy taunted. "Ooooh! Come on, you want some?"

"Cindy liked to intimidate," forensic psychologist Paula Orange said. "She had learned it was better to be a predator than the prey very early on in life. Her early childhood would shape the monster she would become."

Cindy's parents divorced when she was one year old. Her mother would remarry but that would end in divorce as well. She would take care of Cindy and her three sons during the day and go to a waitress job at night.

Cindy stated that she had been raped by an undisclosed family member and by another man who threw her down a flight of stairs after he finished with her.

"Her mother reportedly had different children all by different men," Orange said. "Cindy was molested by one of her mother's endless string of men that she brought into the home."

Cindy would talk about her "rotten" childhood and describe being "raped a few times." She tried to commit suicide on several occasions but that only brought her more frustrations. So instead of harming herself, she decided she would harm others.

"I want them to pay," she said.

By the time she entered Chana High in Auburn, California, Cindy had a well-established reputation of someone who should be feared. Using physical intimidation, she would randomly choose a girl she didn't like and the bullying would begin. She would push and yell, getting in their face. Her victims would be spared no quarter, on one occasion, Cindy ripped the blouse of a girl and forced her to run down the street topless.

"She was a trained bully," Orange said. "She knew exactly how to push the buttons of her victims, strip them of their dignity. It was done to her at home so it was easy for her to pass along the abuse."

Cindy was a menacing presence on campus to the other petite girls. At 5'9" and 140 pounds, she could beat up any girl in the school. She had a strong jawline and broad shoulders but it was her eyes that set her apart from the average bully. Eyes that pierced through her victims and gave them an implicit message.

I want to kill you.

Cindy's crimes would not be limited to physical assaults. She would grab and take whatever she wanted. She would go into liquor stores, stuff food into her pockets and leave. She would go into malls and steal cassette tapes at the record store. After a few months, she graduated to stealing a car. This would land her in a juvenile detention center where she would be a kindred spirit unlike any other she had met before.

LIKE LOOKING INTO A MIRROR

Like Cindy, Shirley Wolf had been the victim of sexual abuse. Her father, Louis Wolf, would rape her. But the abuse didn't stop with just her father. She was a molested by her paternal grandfather and uncle as well.

An observant kindergarten teacher noticed the odd behavior of Shirley and recommended that she get psychiatric help to no avail.

Shirley didn't know where else to turn as she would be abused by all of the men in her life. At the age of six years old, she had run away for the first time. The streets were too rough for her, however, and she was scared back home by the dark characters of Brooklyn.

A lost little girl with nowhere else to go but the house where she was abused.

Her father, Louis, worked as a carpenter but suffered an accident that forced him to take disability. He would remain at home and begin bossing his children around. Then it turned to the sexual abuse of his daughter, Shirley.

When Shirley was around six, the family would move from the east coast to Placerville, California so Louis could be closer to his own family.

Louis Wolf would send Shirley's mother Katherine on an errand to get some groceries one morning. He then locked Shirley's three younger brothers out of the house and turned his attention to Shirley.

He cornered her in the bathroom and raped her.

Shirley would never forgive her father for what he did to her.

Louis would rape his daughter sometimes as much as three times per day. By the time she reached puberty, he put her on birth control.

Shirley never told her mother because she didn't want to break up the family.

Louis would tell Shirley to not tell her mother what he had done. Shirley obliged only because she was afraid how badly the news would hurt her mother.

Eventually, however, the abuse became so intolerable that she told her mother.

Her mother suspected it all along. She then went to the authorities.

Louis would deny that he molested Shirley but plead guilty to reduced charges which brought his sentencing down to a mere one-hundred days.

Louis was told that if he fought the charges, he would be facing fifty years. So he took the three months.

Shirley would then be removed from the home which was her worst fear. She would be bounced from foster home to foster home where she told of feeling "like a stranger."

"You get to the point where you're pushed in a corner and I just came back fighting," Shirley said. "I want to go home. I forgive my father and I try to forget it. He's apologized to me, my family and to God."

A MATCH TO A FLAME

It would be only fitting that the first time the girls would meet, it would be under the guise of violence.

At the detention center, Shirley was being beaten to a pulp by a fellow inmate in the hallway. As per usual, no guards were around. But Cindy stood her ground against the bigger girl, to no avail.

The girl threw her against the wall, punched her in the stomach and twisted her arm.

"Who are you?" Cindy asked as she came upon the two girls fighting.

"Shirley Wolf."

"I like you, Shirley Wolf."

And with that, Cindy got her opponent into a full nelson, easily overpowering Shirley's tormentor.

"Let her have it," Cindy said.

Shirley didn't hesitate. She began pummeling the girl, all of the rage of being abused all of her life came forth as she gave the girl a beat-down.

Cindy threw the girl to the ground and the two laughed as she moaned in pain.

"Later loser," Shirley sniffed.

Cindy laughed. The girl had spunk and they spent the next couple of hours exchanging their life stories.

For some reason, Cindy did not feel hatred toward Shirley. She felt like they had an unspoken bond but she didn't know why.

The truth was, they were both ticking time bombs.

"I think it was an unfortunate chemistry between the two girls," Shirley's defense attorney Thomas Condit said. "I think it also had to do with finding a new friend and wanting to show that she was capable of doing anything that the friend was."

Shirley was the opposite of Cindy in one regard, however, as she did not have Cindy's assurance. Shirley felt "hopeless and helpless" as she talked about running away from the detention center. She talked about this as if it were an impossibility, a faraway dream.

But Cindy felt otherwise. She behaved as if she knew all the answers.

"I can get us out of here," Cindy said with total assurance.

"You can?"

"Sure. I do it all the time. But we're going to need a car. This place where I used to live as all kinds of old people. We can steal one of their cars. But we'll probably have to kill them."

"Yeah," Shirley said.

"You know," Cindy said. "In case one of them rats us out."

Cindy led the way as the girls escaped. They talked about how they would put their sadistic plan in motion. They wanted to find someone old and feeble...someone who could not fight back...someone who they could kill for fun.

"I suppose a good analogy would be to compare the girls to the boys from Columbine who would come over a decade later," Orange said. "One needed the other to pull off such a horrid act. They needed that voice over their shoulder to egg them on. They both wanted the same thing and together they could make it happen."

Both Cindy and Shirley would dye their hair red in order to disguise themselves. They then went "victim hunting," touring Cindy's old neighborhood in Auburn Green, a condo for senior citizens. They wanted a car. A nice one. So they began searching the parking lot for a car and would match the number on the parking slot to the condo number.

Then they would knock on the door. Their questions were innocent. They would ask for directions, a glass of water or ask to use the phone. But there was something about their demeanor, a sinister or insincere look in their eye that set off the alarm bells for all of the senior citizens they met. They were allowed inside by Joe Becker and his wife who gave them a glass of water. When they left, however, the elderly couple immediately washed the glass and scrubbed the phone with alcohol, the girls seemed so dirty.

"They were looking for an easy target," Orange said. "Becker was seventy but still probably too much of a hassle for them. They needed easy."

Then they knocked on the door of Anna Brackett.

"We decided we were going to kill her when we saw her," Shirley said. "She was just an old lady. Just a perfect setup. We killed her because we wanted her car and we didn't want to get caught."

Anna was a retired seamstress who worked for Sears. She had great-grandchildren who were the ages of Cindy and Shirley.

She was a helpful and kind person to all her knew her. She didn't hesitate in helping some girls that were the ages of her great-grandchildren.

"Can I help you?" Anna opened the door with a smile.

"Hi," Cindy said. "Can you please help us? We need to call our parents and the phone down the street is not working."

"Sure," Anna said, opening up her door.

Ann was congenial and didn't see any reason not to trust the girls. She let them into her home and the threesome chatted for over an hour. They sat on the couch and she gave them soda. She would show the girls pictures of her family. Pictures of her children, grandchildren.

"It is unusual for a sociopath to want to know about their victim," Orange said. "They really don't want to know their victim because it humanizes them. So perhaps the teen girls were hesitant at first. But it was more of a case of them working up the nerve to do what they set out to do."

The phone rang and Anna went up to answer it.

The call came from her son.

"I'm on my way," her son said.

"Okay," Anna said, hanging up the phone. "I'm sorry, girls. My son is coming to pick me up. We're going to the bingo parlor."

"Now," Cindy said as the girls pounced.

Shirley grabbed the elderly woman by the throat and slammed her to the ground.

"What are you doing?" Anna screamed. "What are you doing?"

Cindy sprinted to the kitchen and rifled through the drawers. She found a butcher knife and gave it to Shirley.

"Do it," Cindy commanded.

Shirley would then stab the helpless old woman without mercy. She would recall stabbing her in the neck and "freaking out" because the old lady kept screaming.

"You're killing me!" Anna shouted.

"Good," Shirley said, slicing the knife down again. She would stop only when she saw the blood coming out of Anna's mouth.

Anna Brackett would suffer over twenty-eight stab wounds although the coroner believed it could have been more as the blade went through the same entry point. There was one stab wound where the blade had gone in four inches deep past Anna's breastplate.

"She died a horrific death," Orange said. "Painful and horrific. I've read some psychiatrists say that Shirley was getting revenge on all of the people that hurt her in the past, that in some way Anna symbolized her mother and she was killing her mother symbolically. I believe that is psychobabble. Shirley was not that bright. She was following the lead of Cindy and they wanted to kill and maim. That was the point. Not to subconsciously work out her anger. She was a defective unit."

Cindy then sifted through all of Anna's drawers and closets looking for money. They found the keys to the old woman's 1970 Dodge and ripped the two telephones from the wall.

They went into the garage and found out that the keys they had stolen would not start the car. Angered, they left the condo on foot and began hitch-hiking.

Ironically, Anna's son Carl would drive pass them on the street, ignoring the girls who had their thumbs out.

He then entered his mother's home and discovered her mutilated body on the floor.

It was a surreal scene for her son. His mother on the floor in a pool of blood. Trapped in his own real life horror movie, Carl would never have guessed that two underage girls would be capable of such a thing.

LIKE A DAY AT THE OFFICE

Cindy and Shirley made it to her home in Auburn. They turned on the television, eagerly awaiting news of the murder they had committed.

Too many people had spotted them around the neighborhood. In all, eleven people informed the investigating officers of the two red-headed girls with the strange demeanor.

Some remembered Cindy from when she lived with her grandparents in the condo development. The deputies, however, didn't believe that two teenage girls could have done what they did to Anna.

Back home, the girls would cheer as their murder was reported on the evening news.

Then they went to sleep.

At 2:30 a.m. the deputies would arrive at the house of Cindy Collier.

Deputy George Coelho didn't believe the girls did the crime. But after a few minutes of questioning, Shirley confessed.

Cindy, however , would not only confess to the crime, she would gloat.

"She started to laugh," Deputy Coelho said.

Cindy expressed little remorse. She told the deputies that she felt like killing more people.

Shirley was excited and giddy as they had done something that "they had never done before."

They were placed under arrest and one of the deputies began reading her the Miranda rights. Shirley interrupted him, repeating the rights verbatim as she was already familiar with the process.

Cindy would tell the police that she felt jealousy toward anyone who appeared happy and normal. She felt such envy that she wanted to kill them.

The deputy expressed shock as Cindy detailed her desires of wanting to hurt people. She bragged about stabbing, shooting and throwing people into the Auburn Damn. The officers knew it was all bravado...with the exception of what they did to Ann Brackett.

The two girls would go to trial in July of 1983...a juvenile court.

What the girls wanted was fame and publicity.

They would get it as the brutal murder would be talked about in numerous high-profile magazines and the court case would reach a national audience. A movie called "Fun" was produced, chronicling the girl's first day together.

CRIME AND PUNISHMENT

Shirley's attorney, Thomas Condit, would enter a plea of not guilty by reason of insanity. "I'd like to say that Shirley felt sorry," Condit said. "But I can't. That's part of her problem. She told me that while she was killing the old lady, she was thinking of everybody she hated—her father and his mother. But the psychiatrist believes it was a symbolic killing of her own mother."

Both girls would receive the maximum imprisonment for underage girls. They would remain in jail until the age of twenty-five then be released.

"Shirley really can't understand the difference between right and wrong," Condit said. "How do you appreciate right and wrong when you have a father telling you it's wrong not to stay home and service him when you should be in school?"

THE AFTERMATH

Cindy would spend the next nine years at the California Youth Authority facility in Ventura. She would obtain an associate of arts degree then go on to study law at Pepperdine University. She would go on to have four children and live in Northern California without any further brushes with the law.

Shirley would be sent to the Central California Women's Facility near Chowchilla.

She would threaten other inmates and her jailers during her time in prison. She spent her days reading romance novels as she tries to take her mind off the tormented childhood which led her to be capable of such a crime.

"I think of my dad and it hurts," Shirley said. "I'll just feel pain and I'll have to cry to get it out. I can't really pinpoint where it's from. God knows, I'll get hurt and just cry."

Shirley would complete her high school education and become a born-again Christian. The attempts to improve her life would prove futile, however.

She had tried to contact her parents but they never returned her calls or letters. Finally, in the summer of 1992, Shirley tracked down the number of her parents in the Pacific Northwest. Louis, the man who had molested her, would answer her call.

They had not spoken in four years but he had told her that her mother had left him a few months prior, leaving the three young boys with him. Shirley asked about her favorite brother, L.J., but her father avoided giving her a straight answer.

Shirley wanted desperately to know what happened to her younger brother but could not locate him anywhere. Her father would then stop returning her calls.

On June 30th, 1995, Shirley would be freed from prison after serving twelve years for the murder of Anna Brackett.

Her father would die in 2002.

Unlike Cindy, Shirley's life of petty crimes would continue. She would get involved in prostitution, theft, and burglaries. She has shown remorse for the murder but also stated that "there is no going back."

Both women are now free, getting leniency for the crime because of their age. Their light sentences would draw the ire of Anna's son, Carl, who would rage at the judicial system that gave his mother no justice.

KILLER TEEN : THE TRUE STORY OF KRISTINA FETTERS

JANET NIXON

Kristina Fetters was the youngest woman in the state of Iowa to get sentenced to life in prison without parole after she murdered her great-aunt. But eighteen years later she would be re-sentenced after the Supreme Court ruled that mandatory life sentences for minors was unconstitutional.

Kristina would later be released to a hospice center as she developed breast cancer in prison.

But what happened that fateful night of October 25th, 1994? Kristina was only fourteen years old, five-feet tall and barely one hundred pounds. Yet she committed one of the most brutal assaults in the history of her Iowa town.

This is what transpired in her life before and after she committed a brutal murder of her loving aunt.

EARLY LIFE

She was born Kristina Joy Fetters on February 5th, 1980. The product of a biracial union between her mother Darlene and an African-American man, Kristina did not get to know her father growing up.

Instead, she spent her childhood with Arlene and Wayne Klehm. They were the great-aunt and great-uncle of Kristina but she thought of them as her grandparents. She would refer to Wayne as "Uncle Sheenie" and to her aunt Arlene as "Pooper."

Kristina would play at their home as a young child, swinging from bedsheets tied to a tree in the front yard of the couple's one story home.

Wayne was the easy going one of the couple. Arlene, on the other hand, was the one who enforced discipline on the precocious Kristina.

But Kristina was close to her aunt as were all of her other cousins. Arlene was described as a 'spitfire', a woman who spoke her mind.

"Arlene was just a tiny framed, little woman that would tell you exactly where to go and how you could get there," Kristina's cousin Shanna Sickles said.

Kristina would not meet her biological father until she turned eight years old. She wanted a close relationship with him but the bond never materialized.

"I want him in my life," Kristina said to the Iowa Register in 1996. "I need him in my life. I don't think he knows what he wants."

RUNNING WITH A BAD CROWD

Kristina seemed to have little guidance in her early life. At only twelve-years old, she would meet a twenty-three year old African-American man from Milwaukee named Anthony Leon Hoover. He was a gangster "wannabe", seeking membership into a street gang called the "Black Gangster Disciples." Immature and naïve to the perils of the street, Kristina told the man that she was seventeen years old and ran away with him.

But in June of 1993, Hoover would be arrested on kidnapping charges. He held Kristina at gunpoint, broke her nose and then raped her.

Kristina could not cope with the trauma inflicted by the older man. She would not go to school and would runaway on a weekly basis.

By January of 1994, she was so troubled that she was sent to the Orchard Place, an unlocked facility for minors with behavioral problems. Kristin was placed on Prozac and underwent treatment.

"She was on three different medications that are well known to not play well together now," her friend Jaimi Ross said. "She was showing every warning sign, every red flag that you possibly could on these drugs and they were all ignored."

She also sought solace in Christianity to no avail. A Polk County Juvenile Court officer said that Kristina "lived in a fantasy world most of the time."

Her mother, Denise, would support this assessment as she described her daughter as having hallucinatory episodes.

"She'd say 'look, look, there's Johnny. He's laying on the floor," Denise said. "There's a knife in his head. He's bleeding. Somebody help him, somebody help him. And the teachers would try and re-direct her, you know, you need to get up here and finish your homework."

In September of 1994, her Uncle Wayne would die. Aunt Arlene then sent her grand-niece a handwritten letter, trying to smooth things over.

"Let's be nice to each other and forgive me if I hurt you," Arlene Klehm stated in the letter.

But Kristina would not take the olive branch of her great-aunt.

PLOTTING A MURDER

Ten months later, on October 25th, 1994, Kristina and her roommate Jeanie Fox escaped from the Orchard Place.

Their destination was Kristina's great-aunt's home in Polk County, Iowa.

Arlene Klehm was 76-years old and had little contact with her grand-niece since her placement into the mental health facility.

Living in her fantasy world, Kristina concocted the idea that her aunt Arlene had a lot of money. She planned to escape from the facility, kill her aunt and ride off into the sunset in her truck. What her plans were beyond that, she didn't know.

All she knew was that she needed a partner in crime.

First, she approached a girl named Jessica Wilhite. She explained that her aunt had a lot of money and it would be an easy kill. They could take both her money and her truck after doing the deed.

Jessica remained non-committal.

Kristina then went to Tisha Versendaal and told her of her plan.

"She sits in a chair all day," Kristina said. "I'll stab her then cut her throat. She keeps her money in a safe. We'll take all her money then get away in her truck."

But she found no taker in Tish who was due to leave the facility soon. Instead, she settled on Jeanie Fox, who wanted out of the facility.

Telling Jeanie her plan of escaping and leaving the part of killing her aunt out of the equation, the two packed their bags. They left the facility without incident and that is when Kristina told Jeanie of her other plans.

"Do you want to come with me to kill my aunt?" Kristina asked.

A FIELD TRIP TO MURDER

The girls stopped at three different homes before heading off to kill her aunt. The final stop was at the apartment of a friend where Kristina got a small paring knife.

"What do you need that for?" the friend asked.

"I'm going to kill my aunt," Kristina laughed as she left the apartment.

The two girls arrived at Klehm's home and noticed that a van was parked outside.

Her aunt was entertaining company.

Kristina wanted to wait as she didn't want any witnesses.

The two girls then knelt behind a fence and waited for her aunt's friends to leave.

"I am going to fucking kill her," Kristina repeated the sentence like a mantra outside the home. "Satan has given me the power to do so."

Her aunt's visitors finally left and the two impatient girls knocked on the door. The old woman let them both in, unsuspecting of what the girls had in store for her.

The three small-talked in the kitchen before Kristina pulled Jeanie into a side room.

"I'm going to fucking kill her," Kristina said, again like a mantra as if she were psyching herself up.

Gathering up the nerve, Kristina marched into the kitchen where her aunt was sitting and smashed her over the head with a tea kettle.

Arlene fell to the ground. She tried to get up, woozy, and asked what happened.

Kristina showed no mercy. She exchanged the kettle for a heavy metal skillet and smashed it across her aunt's head.

"Give me the knife," Kristina called out to Jeanie.

Taking the paring knife, Kristina tried to slice Arlene's throat but the knife wasn't sharp enough. She then rummaged through the kitchen drawers, found a larger knife and stabbed her aunt in the back.

"Anthony!" Kristina cried out with every stab (according to Jeanie). "Anthony! Anthony!"

"Help!" Arlene wailed at Jeanie who stood and watched. The bloodied woman wobbled over to the phone but Kristina got there first.

"No!" the teen girl said, ripping the phone off the hook.

Kristina would stab her aunt a total of five times in the back. There were also defensive wounds on her hand and lumps on her head.

Her aunt now dead, Kristina wanted a change of clothes. But first she rummaged through Arlene's bedroom, stealing her necklaces and other small pieces of jewelry.

"We need to find her damn keys," Kristina called out to Jeanie.

They searched for the keys to both the safe and the truck to no avail.

Kristina then thought she heard police sirens in the distance. The two girls began to run and Kristina started to cry.

The girls ran down the block, pounding on the doors of neighbors until police arrived.

"I killed my aunt," Kristina sobbed. "I killed my aunt."

"It was a grisly scene," Detective Neil Schwartz recalled as he came upon Arlene's body. "Brutal. Very bloody."

THE AFTERMATH

Kristina would be charged with first-degree murder and her case was transferred from the juvenile system to a district court in order for her to be tried as an adult.

Her defense team would enter a plea of insanity. She would undergo psychiatric examination with Dr. Michael Taylor who stated that he didn't think Kristina was insane but rather had a personality disorder.

Her planning was too precise and her deception upon entering her aunt's house did not suggest that she was insane, the doctor explained. Furthermore, she understood what she had done after the killing.

But another psychiatrist, Dr. Gaylord Nordine, believed that Kristina was in a psychotic state caused by the Prozac. Dr. Taylor disagreed, stating that Prozac would not have had any adverse consequences on her and that Kristina was also on Thorazine at the time which should have made more her even more docile.

"In talking with her I found absolutely no evidence of any type of psychiatric disorder, " Taylor said. "And in talking with her I found absolutely no indication that she was doing anything on October 25, 1994, other than killing her aunt."

On December 18th, 1995, Kristina would be sentenced to life in prison without parole.

She would serve out her sentence at the Iowa Correctional Institution for Women in Mitchellville, Iowa. She would file appeal after appeal as her attorneys would bring up the fact that this was cruel and unusual punishment for a juvenile.

According to her friends, Kristina didn't forgive herself for what she had done.

"When everybody else was telling her that they forgave her and they're showing her unconditional love," Jaimi Ross said. "She didn't feel she deserved it. It was very hard for her to accept."

Kristina and Jaimi would becoming close friends in jail. They had to...They were two children in an adult prison who were serving life sentences.

When other children came into the facility, Kristina and Jaimi would serve as mentors of sorts.

"They came in and everybody would share their story. It would be Kristina, myself, and another inmate. We'd just open ourselves up and let it all pour out and let them see us for the same flawed humans that they are."

A TERMINAL ILLNESS

In 2013, however, Kristina would be diagnosed with inoperable breast cancer. By November of that year, Kristina would be re-sentenced to life in prison with the possibility of parole.

The judge also recommended that she be immediately paroled due to her illness.

The decision on whether or not to set her free set off a firestorm of controversy in Kristina's own family and the state of Iowa.

"To give her her last few moments of joy and peace," Kristina's mother Denise Fetters said. "I think could be the best thing that she could receive."

But other family members weren't so keen on that idea.

"I just don't feel bad for Krissy for where she's at," Kristina's cousin, Shanna Sickles said. "She put herself there. She didn't give my Aunt Arlene the opportunity to die with her loved ones. Bottom line, if you get life in prison without the possibility of parole, it's life."

But Kristina also had her supporters in friend Jaimi Ross.

"I completely understand when people say things like 'Oh, a life for a life, she took a life, she should die in prison,'" Ross said. "That states more about where you're at in life, and not her, not me and not her family. I get that that's where your heart is and that's what you believe. Were not asking for her to have a second chance."

The parole board decided to release Kristina on a hospice-only basis. There was outcry from people who wanted her to stay in jail, stating that the prison only set her free to save on medical costs.

In the end, the bureaucracy mattered little as Kristina had already reached stage four with her cancer.

"No one can alter the past," Kristina's aunt Darcy Olson said. "It is what it is, this happened to our family and it's now time for my family to have closure. Kristina's impending death cannot be denied and while there have been negative comments, we believe, as the victims, our family has suffered enough and we ask the parole board to grant our request."

Darcy was the only family member aside from Kristina's mother that supported her during the trial and parole hearings.

"It's just so bitter sweet," Olson said. "This has been a 19-year old tragedy for my family. This will bring closure for my whole family and help us all cope just a little bit better with the situation."

"Everybody's like, well, she was a monster," Ross said. "She was evil. It would be so easy in this world if that were just the case. But that's not the way that it is. Not everybody that commits a crime...not everybody that's a sinner is evil or a monster. Her legacy, I hope, will challenge other people to see what they can do for kids. For teenagers. Before it gets to the point where they're in prison or needing to go before a judge for any reason."

The cancer would spread throughout her bones and spine. Kristina would live out her last days in pain.

"The screams I had to listen to last Sunday, no mother should ever have to hear in her life," Kristina's mother, Denise said.

Seven months into her release, Kristina would die at the age of thirty-four.

KILLER TEEN NIKKI REYNOLDS

SAMANTHA REED

It is not often that stories appear where we find the perpetrators of violence being children and the victims being parents. Although, scattered throughout history it has been seen that children can be capable of shocking amounts of violence, and many, assuming their innocent nature, fall victim to them. In Coral Springs, Florida in 1997 one such story took place. And still the actions of the evening resonate throughout the community.

In The Beginning

Born in 1979 to a mother that didn't want her, Jacquiline "Nikki" Reynolds was adopted by Robert and Billie Jean Reynolds three months after her birth. The Reynolds were a loving, Christian family from Coral Springs, Florida and they were delighted to welcome their new daughter into their lives.

There was nothing that they wouldn't do for Nikki. Robert Reynolds worked for the Department of Transportation and Billie Jean was an administrative assistant at RJ Reynolds. They had a quiet home and they were devoted to making their daughter happy.

Nikki was a good child. She was devoted to the church, like her parents, and she loved her parents deeply. She would go to the mall with her mother or watch baseball games with her father. She could never spend too much time with them. The Reynolds did everything to ensure that Nikki was being raised in a loving and non-judgmental environment.

Friends and family would agree that the environment was loving, but the Reynolds gave Nikki everything she wanted. She was pampered, she was spoiled, and in the end, she was a bit of a brat. Sometimes the best intentions can have the worst consequences.

Still, Nikki, as she got older, became a good student and didn't act out. She achieved good grades in school and went out of her way to become involved in extra curricular activities. She also stayed heavily involved with the church alongside her parents.

By all appearances, Nikki was the perfect child. She was the child that most parents dream of having and Robert and Billie Jean were delighted with her. But children grow up, despite anything that their parents try to do to stop it, and Nikki was no exception. And not all children grow up in a manner that their parents can be proud of.

The Beginning of the End

Nikki went from being the model child to what most people would call a 'troubled teen'. It didn't start in the way one would expect, with failing grades and a lack of interest in school. It started with a lie, and one that shocked family and friends in the disturbing nature of it.

In 1996, sixteen-year-old Nikki came home from school and claimed that she had been assaulted after getting off of the school bus. Naturally her parents were shocked and appalled to hear that this had happened to her. They immediately called the police to handle the situation officially. Nikki claimed she had been attacked by someone she knew, at first. But when questioned by the police her story quickly changed.

She went on to say that she didn't know her attacker and then that the attack hadn't happened at all. She hadn't been raped. She'd made the whole story up.

Now why would a sixteen-year-old, devote Christian girl make up a story about being raped? Why would she go to the extreme of telling her parents and getting the police involved if it was just a story?

It turns out that Nikki hadn't been raped. Rather she was in a relationship, the first one of a sexual nature in her lifetime, and she was terrified to tell her parents about it. She was worried about what they would think about their daughter sacrificing her morals and her principles just to have a boyfriend. But Carlos Infante was her entire world. The sixteen-year-old classmate was consuming her life focus to the point that she hadn't hesitated to throw caution to the wind.

And when the thought of telling her parents about what was going on had come up, in her mind, fabricating a rape story had seemed like a better idea. Nikki was also concerned that she might be pregnant, a worry that was quickly put to rest, but it also influenced her decision to pursue the rape narrative.

Billie Jean was extremely unhappy with Nikki, potentially for the first time during her parenting of the girl. She didn't like the fact that Nikki had a boyfriend. She didn't like the fact that she'd sacrificed her principles and morals, the beliefs that they thought they'd instilled into her all for some boy. They believed that they'd raised a good, Christian girl and for the first time they were starting to question that belief.

Bille Jean and Robert disliked the idea of Nikki having a boyfriend, it didn't particularly matter who he was. They viewed it as a step down for her. They saw it as a complete abandonment of her belief system, something they had strived to instill in her over the course of her entire life. She was sacrificing everything in order to be with this boy, from their point of view. She was losing herself in him. And Billie Jean and Robert wanted to help get Nikki back on a clear path, on a Christian path.

So, they insisted that she spend less time with Carlos and more time with the church. They hoped that in doing so she would see her wrongdoings and find her true self again. They hoped that in spending more time with the church that she would become closer to the family again and forget about Carlos.

Billie Jean believed that Nikki needed to spend more time with a better group of people, a Christian group of people. She hoped that if Nikki spent time around other good, Christian kids that she would find her way again, that she would find a better crowd. And Billie Jean was willing to go to great lengths to ensure that her daughter found a path that fit with the beliefs and morals of the family.

But sometimes the child, no matter how much they push, cannot realize the hopes and dreams of parents. And sometimes, despite all efforts, things still go wrong.

Rebellion Continues

Teenage rebellion can be a strong force, however, and the more that Billie Jean pushed Nikki to go to church the more she resisted. Nikki said, "I knew that the way I was living was not right in God's eyes, but I did not want to hear all of that." She was too engulfed in her life with Carlos. He was quickly becoming her entire world and nothing else mattered to her. Not her parents, and certainly not her church.

The rebellion was extending into her school life. Nikki, who had once been a good student with marks that her parents could be proud of was now beginning to skip class. Her grades were beginning to fall as a result and she was no longer the academic force that she was before.

It was to the point that Billie Jean and Robert barely recognized the girl that they had raised anymore. Who was this young woman living in their house? She reflected none of the morals and principles they had raised her to uphold. She wouldn't listen to them. She opposed them at every turn. They began to wonder what had happened to their daughter Nikki. Where had she gone?

Nikki went from a happy-go-lucky child that was a pleasure to be around, a child who was soft spoken and loved to go to church to a girl no one could recognize. She wore dark clothes, she changed her music, she changed her bedroom to dark colours – she became the opposite of herself. It was hard to tell if this was simply teenage rebellion or something more going on. Was this all because of Carlos or was there some deeper problem at play?

She slept a lot, more than any teenager should and she isolated herself from her family. Gone were the days of ice cream and base ball games. She no longer went on trips to the mall with her mother. She no longer went to church with her family. She became disinterested in many things that used to hold her attention, things that used to captivate her. Her whole world now revolved around Carlos.

It was her first sexual relationship with anyone in her life and it had reached the point of obsession. She filled her diary with everything to do with Carlos. Her room was plastered with photos of him. Her every waking moment revolved around him. There was an unnatural intensity to her emotions towards him, an unhealthy intensity. And it was quickly becoming evident that this was a problem.

Naturally, Billie Jean and Robert were very concerned about their daughter's current mental state. She was not herself, and the only thing they could blame was Carlos as he was the only changing factor in her life. It seemed that he was a negative influence on Nikki in many ways. He didn't make good grades as a student, and now her grades were plummeting as well.

Billie Jean was also worried that he was coming over every day, potentially when they were at work. They had no way to confirm this, but she didn't like the idea that he was at the house alone with her while they were at work. It didn't sit well with her.

So Billie Jean put her foot down, perhaps for the first time in her experience as a parent. She began to tell Nikki no, especially when it came to Carlos. And Nikki handled it with the maturity level of a toddler as opposed to that of a teenager. Nikki threw awful tantrums. Billie Jean and Nikki would engage in screaming matches in the house that would result in slammed doors. The result was very wearing on Billie Jean. She found herself screaming at Nikki almost all of the time. This was not what she wanted her life as a mother to be. This was not the girl she had raised. She needed to do something about this, but she was at a loss as to what the solution could be.

And despite the screaming matches and the orders to stay away, Nikki still kept seeing Carlos. It seemed that nothing could keep her from Carlos. She would sneak out at night when everyone was asleep to see him and it didn't matter what the consequences were.

Billie Jean's frustration escalated to the point that one day she confided in a friend saying "Don't be surprised if one day you come home and there's police cars and fire trucks up and down the street 'cause one of us, it'll be me or Nikki, but one of us will be gone."

Billie Jean's prediction would prove to hit a little too close to home in the coming days. And the aftermath would shock everyone.

Intervention

It was May 14, 1997 when the school counselor contacted Billie Jean to tell her that there was trouble with Nikki and Carlos. She asked that Billie Jean come in and speak with her in person and that Billie Jean, Robert, and Nikki come in for a full meeting the next day. Upon visiting the high school, the counselor told Billie Jean that Nikki and Carlos had more than just the usual high school relationship issues to deal with.

That day Nikki had told the counselor that she was pregnant with Carlos' baby. This had naturally prompted the counselor to contact Billie Jean immediately about the issue. Billie Jean, having already dealt with Nikki's questionable honesty with the previous rape accusation, was hesitant to believe the pregnancy claim. She was fairly certain that this was another one of Nikki's schemes, but there was a sure way to determine its legitimacy.

So she took Nikki to the drug store to find out what was what.

The results of the pregnancy test were negative. That didn't mean Billie Jean was any less pleased with her daughter. Nikki called Carlos with the news. And despite having a counseling meeting the next day Billie Jean decided to seek guidance from a higher power. She dragged Nikki away from the phone and took Nikki to see the church counselor.

Nikki spoke with her pastor as they waited to see the counselor. He was supportive as he talked to her about her boyfriend problems and offered her guidance. Their conversation with the counselor did not have the same supportive tone. The counselor spent the session telling Nikki that her mother did not deserve the behaviour she was displaying. She raised her voice and yelled at Nikki. This didn't go over very well.

Nikki removed herself from the office and from the church. She wanted nothing more to do with the impromptu counseling session. And as she stood in the parking lot of the church she even debated removing herself from the family by running away. But she didn't run away, however. Instead, she took a higher ground, something that hadn't been seen from her in almost a year. She went back into the counselor's office and apologized to her mother. And she finished the session with the counselor before returning home with her mother.

Billie Jean believed that they had made a step in the right direction. She would be the one to learn how wrong she was about that fact.

Confusion and Confessions

It was barely an hour after their visit to the counselor on May 14, 1997 that the call came in to 911. At 7:07pm Nikki Reynolds' panicked voice came over the phone saying "I stabbed her repeatedly in the back. There's blood all over her and all over the floor and everything."

Police were at her house in minutes and the scene that they witnessed was one that would stay with some of the officers for years after. When police arrived they found Nikki waiting on her doorstep. One of the officers who responded indicated that "She had blood all over, blood on her legs, blood on her face."

Nikki was placed in the back of the police car and left to wait while the police went to investigate. A tape recorder was left on with her in the police car so that anything that was said while she was alone was recorded and on file. It recorded her praying that her mother was still be alive and saying that she had learned her lesson. She was asking God to forgive her and for her mother to please still be alive.

Her mother was brought out of the house on a stretcher by the EMTs and she was still alive at the time that she left the house. However, Billie Jean was pronounced dead at the hospital at 8:10pm after suffering from 13 stab wounds.

Nikki was taken to the police department immediately. Robert came home from work to find the house in a state of chaos, surrounded by police cars and police tape. He hadn't yet been informed of the situation that had come to pass behind the front doors of his home. He broke down at the news that his wife was gone and that his daughter was responsible. The shock of it was something that he couldn't quite comprehend.

The scene inside the house was gruesome and shocking to police investigators. It depicted Billie Jean's terrible, drawn out death as she fought to get away from her daughter. But there was no escape for her as she was stabbed repeatedly until she finally lay immobile on the floor.

The police found the kitchen knife that had been used as the murder weapon in the sink and it still had blood on it. They also found evidence that someone, likely Nikki, had attempted to clean up the scene using towels and dishcloths. The blood soaked pieces of cloth were scattered about the kitchen unable to handle the sheer amount of blood that had resulted from the incident.

While the police officers worked diligently at the crime seen the detectives questioned Nikki about the murder. And it didn't take too much effort to get her to talk.

"I didn't have any intentions of lying." Nikki said. "I didn't have any secrets. I wanted to get it out." She felt almost compelled to tell the story of what had happened. She needed to let them know.

"It was simple, all I had to ask her was what happened today and just started chatting. She went through the whole story from a to b," said the detective who interviewed Nikki.

The story that was told by Nikki revolved heavily around Carlos Infante, the infamous boyfriend. Nikki had used her fake pregnancy to keep Carlos in a relationship with her when he wanted to leave, fearing what would happen if he left. When she had found out she was not pregnant, for sure, she called him to give the news. Carlos indicated that he wanted nothing to do with her and all of her lies. He'd had enough. Billie Jean had even got on the phone with Carlos and apologized for all of the drama that he'd had to endure at the hands of her daughter.

Nikki had decided then and there that someone would die that day. She even took a handful of aspirin before going to the counseling meeting with her mother at the church. She was certain that she could overdose on it. She was certain that it would be her that would die.

However, when the overdose failed her thoughts went from suicide to homicide rather quickly. But the intended victim had not been her mother.

Her plan had been to get a hold of Carlos the next day and kill him. She figured she could catch him after first hour and slash his throat if she snuck up behind him. She believed that if she couldn't have him then no one should be allowed to have him. He belonged to her essentially.

However, the one obstacle in her plan to kill Carlos was the meeting they had with the guidance counselor the next day. Nikki was unsure whether she would be sent home after the meeting or not. In order to kill Carlos she would have to skip the guidance meeting. So, in order to accomplish this, she figured she would have to kill her parents as well. She would just wait until they were sleeping and then simply slash their throats. Then they could no longer stand in her way.

A real obstacle came into this metaphorical plan when her father left for church after dinner that night alone and her mother stayed home. This was very out of character for them. Nikki also stayed home as her mother told her she was grounded for the rest of the evening. She was instructed to clean the dishes after dinner.

Nikki decided that she would just roll with this change. She believed, since she was now home alone with her mother, that it would be much easier to kill her mother now, clean up the mess, and then wait until her father returned. She could then kill him and do the same. Finally, she could drive herself to school in the morning, wait for

Carlos, and kill him after first hour just like she had planned. It would work out perfectly.

Logical thought was gone at this point in time. Nikki was acting strictly on whatever thoughts came to her mind and they were frantic, desperate. Still, she waited for her opportunity to arrive. She waited for her moment when she could kill her mother.

Opportunity came while she was cleaning up in the kitchen and Billie Jean was working at her computer. Nikki took a kitchen knife, paused for a moment to check the blade for its sharpness, and then slowly approached her mother. She hesitated now that she had the knife in hand. She wasn't sure what it would feel like to slash someone's throat.

When she finally got up the nerve to come up behind her mother and attempt to cut her throat it didn't slash it, it only cut it. Billie Jean jumped up in surprise and darted towards the laundry room. She screamed, "No, Nikki, no."

"I told her I had to kill her because I can't live without Carlos," Nikki explained to police in her interview.

Nikki kept stabbing her because she wanted to put her out of her misery, she claims. She didn't want her mother to suffering any longer. And in her last moments, Billie Jean still offered her daughter forgiveness for killing her.

Nikki spent one night in the hospital because of her claim of ingesting a large amount of Aspirin. After that she was turned over to the county jail where she was formally booked on a charge of First Degree Murder.

The First Trial

The first trial for Nikki Reynolds lasted from April 14, 1999 – May 3, 1999.

If convicted, Nikki faced life in prison after spending two years in a Juvenile Detention Centre. The prosecution built their case around Nikki's obsession with Carlos Infante, making sure to indicate that he was not at fault in any way and rather he was also one of the three listed on Nikki's kill list.

The defence opted to take an insanity plea route, rather than try to dispute the charge that Nikki had committed the murder – something she had confessed to multiple times. This defence fell flat. The criterion for an insanity plea is very strict. The accused has to suffer from a serious mental illness and the accused has to be unaware that what they are doing is wrong or has consequences.

The psychologist that testified for the prosecution indicated that Nikki was well aware of what she was doing, and rather that she was just a confused girl. The defence tried to argue that Nikki suffered from Borderline Personality disorder. They claimed that individuals suffering from this disorder could idolize the individuals they are with and then suddenly snap, and become violent. Which is very similar to Nikki's reaction after Carlos indicated he wanted nothing to do with her. They also claimed that the Aspirin played a part as Aspirin can cause metabolic imbalances and psychosis upon overdoes.

Regardless of the claims on either side, the jury was hung and the trial ended in a mistrial.

The Second Trial

Second trail for Nikki Reynolds began on Sept 1, 1999.

Similar to the first, the prosecution brought a series of psychologists to the stand to prove that, while not a rational act, Nikki was not insane. The prosecution also claimed that her mother's death was premeditated.

The defence countered that Nikki was mentally ill and called experts to speak to Nikki's sanity. The defence also brought forward Nikki's biological mother to testify. The birth mother had a long history of mental illness and family violence. The defence argued that it was the anxiety over losing Carlos that pushed Nikki over the edge and brought her mental illness to the surface.

After much deliberation, Nikki Reynolds was found guilty of Second Degree Murder at the end of the trial.

At the sentencing hearing on January 7, 2000 Nikki's biological mother made a plea to include treatment as a part of Nikki's sentence. She believed that her daughter needed help, much like she had needed help in her lifetime.

Nikki also addressed the court, pleading with the judge to sentence her to a psychiatric facility instead of prison. She truly believed that there had been something wrong that day, if not insanity, than something else. She believed that she needed help. She bore no ill will towards her family. She hated none of them. She had never hated them and still didn't.

However, the judge believed that the wrongness of what she had done to outweigh all else. He gave her the maximum sentence under Florida law, 34 years in prison. She was resentenced to 21 years and 8 months on April 4, 2001 due to a change in sentencing laws in the state of Florida.

In the end Robert Reynolds remarried in 1998 and has had no contact with his daughter since she was sent to prison on January 2000.

And Nikki was incarcerated at the Gadsden Correctional Facility in Quincy, Florida. She was eligible for parole in 2015 and was released.

SANDRA BRIDEWELL

THE BLACK WIDOW

PAUL BIRD

Some people are desperately unlucky. Misfortune follows them, leeching into every part of their lives. And just when it seems that matters might be turning for the better, it strikes again. Others contribute to their own personal tragedies, individual actions steering their lives, like a mis-programmed driverless car, towards their own downfalls.

Which of these destinies applies most to Sandra Bridewell depends very much on your own perspective, your personal interpretations of the facts, of the suggestions, of the outcomes. But the sobriquet 'The Black Widow' gives a clear idea of where many stand in their interpretation of her life choices.

Yet there are two sides to every story. Our early lives shape us, and it certainly seems to be the case that Sandra's formative years were troubled. The extent to which those uncertain times contributed to her later path is again up to the individual to decide. Sandra Bridewell was adopted shortly after she was born in April 1944, and her birth parents remain unknown. Her new parents were Camille and Arthur Powers, of Sedalia, Missouri. Those first few years were good. Sandra was loved by both parents and life was comfortable. Arthur managed a packaging plant, where Dr Pepper soda was pumped into bottles ready for sale. Camille was a typical post-war housewife.

Whether absence from her biological parents pitted those early years we can but guess, but certainly what happened when Sandra was just three years old would play a significant part in her future and turn what had been a relatively normal childhood into years of unhappiness.

Camille was killed in a car accident. Arthur was devastated. Suddenly alone, with the responsibility of a toddler to raise, his life turned upside down. The impact on young Sandra can only have been considerable. In the end her father decided that a new start was essential. He gave up the bottling plant and moved to Oak Cliff, Texas, a pleasant suburb of Dallas, where he remarried.

He moved from manufacturing to sales, working as a salesman of cemetery plots. Sandra was young enough to adapt to her new life in some respects, but in one major way, she failed to adjust at all. It was not really her own fault. Her new stepmother, Doris, was – according to Sandra at least, and that is something (given what we will soon learn) that needs to be treated with caution – a stepmother of fairy tale evilness.

The two failed to develop any kind of relationship. With Arthur working long hours and often away, tensions between the females in his life grew more intense with every passing year. Doris could not accept her new daughter, was jealous of the affection she drew from Arthur. In turn, Sandra never made a bond with her new mother. After all, this was the third woman in her young life to take on the role of principal carer. Firstly, and briefly, had been her birth mother, then Camille had provided a blip of happiness. But now it was down to Doris. And she did not care about her daughter at all.

According to what Sandra would later claim, those early years were full of woe. Doris refused to allow friends over for birthday parties or sleepovers. The result was that Sandra found it hard to build close relationships with her peers. She would fight incessantly with her mother, often resulting in Sandra finding herself locked in a dark closet as a punishment.

Perhaps worse of all, Doris would know how to hit the most sensitive nerves in her young daughter. She would tell her that nobody loved her, nobody cared for her and nobody wanted her. If such treatment was the case, then it inevitably that behaviour must have played a role in the making of Sandra Bridewell. Her self-confidence, self-esteem and self-belief were shattered. She became needy and dependent, yet also manipulative. Classmates tell of how, as a young woman, she developed a well formulated process for attracting men.

She would adopt – perhaps the term is unfair, it could have been her real self – the persona of a helpless victim. A woman apparently skilled socially but vulnerable. Soon, her tactics would deliver more than just a succession of boyfriends.

After completing High School – she graduated in 1962 - Sandra attended college without committing to her education and, after a year, dropped out. It seemed to those who knew her at the time that her intention was simple. To secure a husband.

But, they felt, she did not want a man for love, or security or to provide her with emotional comfort. No, the men she sought had one thing in common. And that was to do with the number of dollar bills they possessed. 'She had a way with men, they were fascinated with her,' recalled a childhood friend when Sandra's criminal case was hitting the headlines many years later.

Indeed, Sandra fabricated a number of stories about her early life. Perhaps because it had been so unhappy, or maybe because she liked it that her lies earned her attention, the tales of her upbringing varied depending on who she was with at the time. Sympathy would be evoked when she claimed that both her adoptive parents had been killed.

On other occasions a different tale she loved to tell was that her parents were wealthy Irish aristocrats. She would also reveal another tragedy in her life, the falsehood of a successful boyfriend who appeared to have it all, Westpoint, money...but who had committed suicide, shooting himself while she looked on, aghast but helpless.

For all her tales and troubles, Sandra soon appeared to find happiness – or money. Maybe both. She met David Stegall, a successful, high-end dentist who was born and bred in Los Angeles and had a number of celebrities among his clientele. Now living in Dallas, he enjoyed a sprawling house, loved his flash cars and was attracted to beautiful women. Sandra certainly fitted that last category. Dark haired, slim with a perfect face, she was the text book wife. Her seductive charms quickly won Stegall over.

The two married and three daughters quickly followed. It seemed, on the surface, an ideal marriage. The 1960s were in full swing and the young family could have been on the cover of any lifestyle magazine. But as is often the case, what appeared to be so idyllic from the outside was covering a troubled core. That maelstrom centred on Sandra's spending. Her lifestyle was so extravagant that she drained her husband dry.

The marriage lasted nearly thirteen years, but by the mid-1970s even Stegall's salary was no match for the speed in which his wife went through money. He fell into serious debt, being forced to borrow heavily from his father to meet her financial commitments and save their house. The pressure was intense, and soon the story of the Westpoint boyfriend was being mirrored in reality. Sandra found her husband in a closet, with a gun pointed at his head. She talked him out of suicide, but he survived only a few weeks. A second suicide attempt was successful, and Stegall was discovered on his bed, his wrists slashed, and his head blasted open with a shotgun wound.

No suspicion fell on Sandra and the loving wife, to the outside world at least, had encountered yet another tragedy in her short but rollercoaster life. She was just thirty-one years old.

Stegall was well insured. The money covered his, or more accurately her, debts, and the newly widowed thirty-something sold her late husband's practice and found herself again able to spend as freely as she wished. Once more she turned on her charms and went on the look-out for eligible men, meeting several and dating many. Soon, she met a Dallas property developer called Bobby Bridewell. He was well known in the area, and very rich. They married, Bridewell officially adopting her three daughters as his own, and they settled in a large and comfortable house, living in one of the most affluent parts of Dallas.

Yet tragedy remained a regular visitor to Sandra Bridewell's door. While this time no suspicion at all could fall on her for the events that ensued, her own behaviour did little to evoke sympathy among those who knew her or, when matters escalated later, the public and media as a whole.

Bobby Bridewell developed cancer, and his health went downhill rapidly. It seems as though the circumstances hit Sandra hard, but not hard enough to stop her moving him out of the house to live with a friend so she could have it re-designed to her taste. Bobby died while staying with the friend, and husband number two had passed.

It was after Bobby's death that matters became more sinister. Sandra befriended her late husband's oncologist, Dr John Bagwell, and his wife. John and Betsy welcomed the grieving woman into their lives and went out of their way to be warm and helpful. But their kindness was exploited, and soon they began to weary of the constant unexpected visits – Sandra even turned up in New Mexico where the couple were holidaying. Requests for childcare were at first happily met, then reluctantly accepted until eventually they felt that they had to put their foot down. John and Betsy, after all, had their own lives to lead.

Yet, inexplicably, on June 16th 1982, Betsy was found in an airport parking lot, she had been shot in the head with a stolen gun; apparently, it was suicide. The story, though, is far more complex and disturbing than even this. Why would the wife of a successful doctor, in an apparently happy marriage, kill herself? And, why had there been no suicide note? Later, a privately funded investigation would throw doubt onto the entire suicide theory.

It transpired that the last person to see Betsy alive had been Sandra Bridewell. She had asked for Betsy to drive her to the hospital to hire a car, as her own had broken down. Then, Sandra realised that she had left her licence in her own car, and Betsy drove her back to this before once again returning to the hospital. She was never seen alive again.

Many doubts existed over the whole affair, but the police settled on suicide, and would not re-open the case.

Sandra was forty-one when she first met her the man who would become her third husband. Alan Rehrig was eleven years her junior and had just moved into the area after getting a new job working for a mortgage company. He was driving around, looking for a place to live when he spied Sandra in her yard. He stopped to ask if she knew of any apartments that might be suitable for a young, single man and she agreed to help him look.

The newcomer to town was a man looking to settle down. Like so many college sports stars – he had been a fine athlete – Rehrig had struggled to make the move from college hero to successful adult. First, he'd tried a career as a golf professional, but earning a living as a sportsman requires considerable talent and although good, he did not possess the necessary edge to really reach the big time. Next, a dabble in the growing local oil business also failed to bring returns.

So, when his pal from way back, Phil Askew, was looking to extend his own mortgage business, Rehrig leapt at the opportunity. Askew said later: 'We were looking at adding a few people, so I said, "Why don't you come on down here, and we'll give it a try.' Askew recalled the speed with which Rehrig took his chance. 'I think he was down here the next week.'

Sandra Bridewell and Rehrig quickly became close, and Rehrig was great with her own kids. His mother, Gloria, explained the relationship, and the physical attraction her son felt for the older woman. 'He thought she was beautiful,' she said. But the relationship was once more based on Sandra's lies; she claimed to be just 36, then came an even bigger untruth. She turned up at his office one day and announced that she was pregnant, with twins. What Rehrig did not know was that such an outcome was impossible. Sandra had needed a hysterectomy some years before and was unable to have children. Yet both Alan Rehrig and his mother were completely taken in by the stories his lover told. 'We felt sorry for her', said the older woman later, 'He felt like he had something to offer her with his family, and she just embraced us like we were going to be her saviours.' In fact. Sandra was simply applying her standard tactic, that of playing the poor little rich girl. Rehrig's friend, Carl McKinney, offers more of the story telling of a time the two of them collected him for an outing.

'He picked me up in a Mercedes Benz that she owned. Well, she sat on the console next to him' McKinney told NBC news at the time of Bridewell's trial in 2008. 'She hung on to him while he drove.' McKinney was taken in by her allure as well, envying his friend the beautiful woman who seemed to adore him.

Rehrig was in love, although a little worried by the speed at which matters were moving, and the couple were married by the end of the year. The final rivet to seal her ambition was the 'news' that she had 'miscarried' and lost their twins. How could she not be treated with love and sympathy after enduring such an ordeal?

It was a short-lived liaison. This time, Sandra did not wait before spending her new husband dry. 'She can get through $20000 a month!' he once told friends. She also persuaded him to take out a large insurance policy on his life.

Rehrig soon had seen enough, and in under a year he separated from his new wife, moving in with the same friend, Phil Askew, who had given him the job with his mortgage company. But Sandra was not going to let go that easily. She contacted him within a couple of weeks and said that they needed to talk. They agreed to meet at a storage depot – each had placed some of their possessions there when they moved into their shared house.

Askew picked up the story. 'I was pulling into the driveway, and he was pulling out. I waved at him, and he waved at me. That's the last I saw him.'

Askew thought no more of it until, a few hours later, he received a call from Sandra. She stated that her estranged husband had not shown up, which she said was typical of his behaviour. Although Askew told her that he had left for the meeting, she said that she would not wait any longer and was heading home. Alan Rehrig failed to return to either Askew's house, or his own, that night.

Next, Sandra hired a private investigator, William Dear. Rehrig's friends assumed it was to help find her missing husband but in fact it was to protect her from him, she maintained. Dear told NBC that, according to Sandra, there had been an incident which had scared her badly. She had been water skiing behind Alan's boat when he had made a sudden, unexpected and violent turn. The force of the change in direction had thrown her off her skis and into the water. Then he had left her struggling in the lake. She was, she had told Dear, afraid for her life.

Perhaps that explained why she would not report Rehrig missing to the local police when he failed to show for their meeting and was not seen in the days that followed. Or, the reason could be more sinister. People would later wonder whether the move to get her home protected from a would-be killer husband was no more than a cynical ploy to remove suspicion from herself. That was one of the problems with Sandra Bridewell, nothing she said, or did, could really be taken at face value.

The next time Rehrig was seen, he was dead. Shot in the head and chest, he was discovered slumped in his Ford Bronco in Oklahoma.

Sandra was a suspect...but only if indeed a crime had been committed. She alternated between playing the poor, but proper, lady; the victim of life's tempests on the one hand and completely refusing to answer questions on the other. In the end, there was nothing investigators could do but let her go. Their plan had been to question the not very grieving three-time widow further but when she hired some high-powered Dallas lawyers they made it clear to the police that they should either charge their new client or leave her alone. It made Pacheco even more suspicious. Surely, the almost certain murder of a husband, even one to whom marriage was shaky, would make a person want to know the truth? Therefore, would they not help the police with their enquiries to the greatest extent that they could?

Pacheco held the firm belief that Sandra was Rehrig's killer. Perhaps the crime was committed simply to get her hands on the insurance policy he had recently taken out; perhaps the motive was fear – fear of her husband, or maybe just a fear that, if they divorced, he would get some of her estate. Yet the facts were skimpy; consisting of little more than hearsay and speculation. It was the case that Sandra could have shot him when they met at the storage lot – but she denied that he ever turned up. Yes, their limited evidence pointed to the fact that Rehrig's six feet one-inch frame was behind the steering wheel when he was shot, and the seat was much further forward when the car was found, suggesting that he had been shot elsewhere and driven to Oklahoma. Sandra Bridewell was only five feet three inches but being shorter than a husband is not evidence of murder.

True, Rehrig was dressed for warmer climes than chilly Oklahoma, wearing just a t shirt and shorts when discovered in freezing conditions. Dallas was substantially warmer than the more northern city but having a higher temperature does not make a place the definite site of a crime. Certainly, Sandra's alibi gave a window of opportunity, over night, when she could have returned to the car and driven it north before coming home, perhaps by coach or train, to Dallas. But lack of an alibi does not point to murder.

The lawyers had won, and there was nothing at all Steve Pacheco and his fellow investigators could do other than to end their enquiries into Sandra's role in her husband's death, whatever their suspicions might otherwise tell them.

Sandra might have appeared to mourn deeply over the loss of her second husband, Bobby Bridewell, but she had no such pretensions with regards to Rehrig. She was late for his funeral, where he was buried with the minimum of fuss in the cheapest way possible. She even got friends to meet those costs, such as they were. Meanwhile, she was banking the $220000 insurance money his policy delivered. Then again, this third marriage was breaking down, she did claim to have been scared by Rehrig's behaviour, and she had seen herself as a suspect – deserved or otherwise – in his murder. Perhaps she had reason to be less than devastated by his death.

A friend from the time, Barbara Nathan, offered a little perspective on Sandra's behaviour: 'She was a little flirty. So were some of the men, I might add,' she said. It is not hard to imagine the impact this striking lady in the open topped Mercedes from the best zip code in Dallas could have on many men. They were flattered by her attention, lured by her charms.

But although she was free, and wealthy, Sandra appeared to have gone too far this time. Losing one husband to death might be unfortunate, a second careless but a third is downright suspicious – add to that mysterious circumstances surrounding the suicide of her friend and people were beginning to talk. Then, a local magazine published an article highlighting the mysterious circumstances that seemed to follow Sandra like a particularly virulent form of the plague – a variety from which she was immune but that seemed to attack her friends and lovers with impunity.

She moved with her family from Dallas and headed to the liberal Californian city of San Francisco. There, she established 'friendships' with a number of men who, in return for her attentions and apparent lack on inhibition when it came to the bedroom, were prepared to offer her gifts and, sometimes, substantial loans. One of $23000 was soon surpassed by another of $70000. In both of these cases the victims tried to get their money back through the courts, but Sandra Bridewell had a way of avoiding retribution.

The US is a big place, and as soon as stories began to close in on her Sandra would move to other States, catching victims on the way. She managed to find homes in Hawaii, Boston and Connecticut, the wealthy owners easily duped by her charms. But Sandra Bridewell's selfishness then began to take on new depths. Firstly, she sought to use religion as a way into men's wallets. She pretended to be a missionary who travelled the world working with orphans from the poorest parts of the globe. Meanwhile, she became less circumspect about her attempts to secure money; she took on the social security numbers of other people and used these to get hold of credit cards which she would then spend out, with not a single intention of paying anything back. Even more despicably, she used her daughters' credit history to extend her own spending. All three of her children were sent into spiralling debt.

As the web closed in on the soon to be named Black Widow, Bridewell changed her name, using her adoptive mother's name of Camille; later she would drop the central 'e' in her surname to become Bridwell. Perhaps she realised that her actions were soon to catch up with her.

By 2006 Sandra Bridewell was living in North Carolina and using yet another false name, this time Camille Bowers. She had moved in as a kind of glamourous housekeeper to look after a wealthy but elderly woman called Sue Mosely. Sandra had reached a deal with Sue's son, Jim, that she would look after the housekeeping, cleaning and so forth in return for free board and lodging in the luxurious home.

For Sandra, it was too good an opportunity to miss. A trusted position living with an elderly lady with loads of money! Very soon social security checks were making their way to her account, mortgage payments were being diverted and she gained ready access to Sue Moseley's bank details. But Jim became suspicious, did some research leading him to finally finding a lengthy newspaper report on his mother's housekeeper's previous life. He went to the police with his suspicions and agreed to act as the front man in a sting.

It led to Sandra Bridewell's arrest, and subsequent conviction for fraud, identify theft, theft and was sentenced to two years in prison, along with a huge fine of $250000. But the police remained suspicious that she had done more, and the case into the death of Alan Rehrig was reopened.

Was Sarah Bridewell the culprit? It is something we may never properly discover. For local police officer Steve Pacheco, it remains unfinished business. 'It's the case that I'll never forget,' he said 'I wish it was solved. I mean, it will never go away.'

Back in the 1980s, when he was investigating the crime, he received an anonymous call from Dallas. This communication, from a woman who is still unidentified, told Sandra's full story, contagious warts and all. But to what extent could it be believed? As outwardly pleasant as she might have seemed to the dinner party and tennis set of wealthy women who lived around her, she never really fitted in. She was a bit of a loner, polite but reserved. And there was always the lingering suspicion that she was on the prowl, that the husbands who provided these women with their enviable lifestyles could be led astray by the dark-haired woman. Lured into her web, as it might be said. Could the stories and suspicions regarding Sandra be no more than exaggerations and the bitter outpourings of an envious woman?

Rehrig's friend, Carl McKinney, tried to put the change in his friend's life in some kind of perspective. To McKinney, that first sight of Sandra Bridewell was crucial. 'When he drove up and saw her, he was just mesmerised,' said McKinney of his friend. 'I think it was: "Wow! Look at this lady." But hooking a husband is not a crime. And although we know that the **B**lack Widow did break the law, in an odious and vicious way, there is a difference between fraud – even when it involves robbing a vulnerable old lady – and murder.

Perhaps the adopted girl with the terrible childhood was the victim of tragedies which saw the deaths of three husbands and a close friend. Perhaps she just had an unlucky life, her own wrongful acts of fraud stimulated by a very difficult upbringing where she never had the chance to feel wanted in her new family.

Or, perhaps that is not the case at all. Perhaps the black widow lived up to its reputation as one of the most efficient killers in the entire animal kingdom. Its bite is deadly, its poison lethal.

BLACK WIDOW : The True Story of DENA THOMPSON

151

BRIANNA WELLS

Dena Thompson is a woman who held power over every man that had the misfortune of falling for her charms.

Dubbed a psychopath, Dena succeeded in fooling everyone around her, including investigators, with her lies and charm for over twenty years.

Dena would post to Lonely Hearts columns and lure a steady stream of lovers and husbands into her world, eventually leaving each one emotionally and financially bankrupt.

Her first husband lost everything to her and wound up as a desperate man on the run from a mafia threat that did not exist. With one husband gone and his money spent, Thompson would go on to bigamously marry Julian Webb, a successful advertising salesman. In three short years, Mr. Webb would be found dead in his bed from an unexplainable drug overdose. Thompson's third and final husband would soon be fighting for his life when she suddenly attacked him with a bat. Still, somehow, this master manipulator would convince an entire jury that she was nothing less than the victim of abuse. No matter how many fruitless chases she sent investigators on, Thompson would not be able to keep the family members and friends of her victims from stringing the pieces together one at a time.

Her crimes were finally brought into the light of day and she would be imprisoned for her killings.

EARLY LIFE

Dena Thompson was born Dena Holmes in 1960 to a lower middle class family from Hendon, London. Her parents were named Michael and Margaret Holmes. Her father had previously worked as a prison officer but had since retired, and her mother lived as a housewife. Her childhood and teenage years held no indication of unhappiness or abuse and she graduated from school with the highest marks. Her life moved by uneventfully until, at the age of 22, she began a career with the Woolwich building society and met Lee Wyatt on a blind date set up by his cousin, Bob Reed, in 1982. On October 12th the following year, the two married in a registry office and moved into a house just below the South Downs. A small village, Dena and Lee's neighbors describe the quaint area as a "very friendly, happy place to live."

Jackie Howells, a neighbor, described the two, saying: "They were ok. You know, just ordinary neighbors when they first moved here."

Pete Howells, Jackie's husband, recalled that Mr. Wyatt was a relatively private man. "Lee kept himself to himself. You know, [polite] enough to say good morning, um, the usual things, but he was never there long enough to build up a conversation with."

Five years later, in 1987, the seemingly happy couple brought a son into the world named Darren.

Lee was an avid toy enthusiast and established the Denalee Crafts company, combining both of their names. The company would distribute hard and soft toys successfully for a time.

For extra income, Dena continued her second job working for the Woolwich building society in Arundel. Taking inspiration from the success of popular cartoon characters and the money behind merchandising, Lee worked to make his fortune by developing a soft toy character for use in cartoon films.

Their shared endeavor would prove not to be the life changing decision they thought it to be, however, when the firm went belly up and Lee was forced to allow his father-in-law to set him up with a new job at the Bedford Hotel in Brighton. Little did Lee know, that this business failure would flip a previously unseen switch in Dena's heart, hurtling her down a dark path of sex, fraud, bigamy, and murder.

Realizing that her seemingly imminent riches were gone before they began, Dena got her first taste of fraud when she began helping herself to the first installments of 26,000 pounds from the Woolwich building society. At the same time, she began to cast her eyes outward for a new man that could bring her success where she felt her current husband had failed. She soon met and began a passionate affair with Julian Webb, whom she met when he visited her office to sell advertising for the West Sussex Gazette.

Julian put forward the idea of doing a makeover using make up and clothing from local businesses in order to bring in customers. At Julian's suggestion, Dena became the model for this idea, and she was very much in love with the new work.

Julian was an active man, an avid bodybuilder and fisherman until he began a relationship with Dena. Soon, his only hobby was to please his new woman.

Peter Howells describes the moment he first saw Dena with Julian , saying: "One day, looking out the back door, [I] just happened to see Dena and another man kissing on the back doorstep, which was rather strange to say the least."

Dena loved the adrenaline rush of both stealing money and cheating on her husband. It was like a drug for her and attaining this kind of "high" would go on to dominate every action she took for the rest of her adult life.

OUT WITH THE OLD, IN WITH THE NEW

Rosemary Webb, Julian's mother, knew very little about Dena when she and Julian came to her with the announcement that they wanted to marry. Understandably, Rosemary was "a bit taken aback at the speed of this, as they'd only met last May," and they had announced their intentions in August of the same year. Only a fortnight later, wedding cards could be seen decorating the front windows of Dena's home. Neighbors were more than a little confused, since Dena Wyatt was already married. No one had seen Lee in weeks and it was as if he disappeared off the face of the earth.

Julian and Dena married on December 2nd, 1991, and Julian did not know that the marriage was bigamous.

Without Julian's knowledge, Dena had sent her first husband running for the hills only months before their marriage. Dena and Lee had signed up for the mortgage on their home together in Yapton, West Sussex. Three months later, in the year of 1991, Denawould give her husband stunning news. She claimed the two needed to separate because Lee was about to come into a large fortune, as there was allegedly a multi-million dollar deal being set up with Walt Disney over his stuffed toy named "Shaun the Leprechaun."

She told him that the mafia was now out to kill him for a cut of the money.

In order to make the lie more believable to Lee, as well as their friends and family, Dena forged letterheads from well-known toy company in the U.S. and showed them to her husband, writing up a lucrative contract that only required his signature.

Lee fell so completely for the deception that he quit his job at the Bedford Hotel.

On June 30th, a debt collector appeared at the door. Dena told her husband to run for his life while she intercepted the man. Lee would run out the back door, praying he would get away unscathed.

Fearing for his family's well-being, Lee Wyatt went on the lamb, but Dena would not allow him to fully disappear without also convincing him to write a series of letters framing himself for the Woolwich building society fraud as she continued to steal more and more money through false accounts.

In an interview taken years later, Lee was quoted saying: "She lives a life of lies and fantasy, and I was the mug who went along with it."

Lee Wyatt gave himself a new name after going on the lamb, Collin Mitchel, and sought work in the Cornish seaside resort of Newquay.

The man that eventually gave him work, David Rodd, was the manager of Carousel Amusements. He stated that Lee came in "to get away from his life in West Sussex, which was nothing strange at the time because a lot of people work for the summer, or something like that." Employees described the mysterious man as easy going and easy to talk to, happy to go out with coworkers for drinks. The job even came with a flat above the establishment that Lee rented for a place to stay. When coworkers eventually learned of his true identity much later, they were more than a little shocked.

A coworker, Mark Pope, laughed about the absurdity of such a sudden revelation, stating in an interview: "Maybe that's why when we were shouting 'Collin' he wasn't replying. We thought he might have been a little bit deaf."

For three years, Lee hid from the invisible boogeymen his cheating wife had created.

Dena, on the other end, set up shop with Julian in the house that Lee had purchased.

Lee sent most of the money he earned to his wife while he lived as a vagrant, believing that any moment his wife would call him, let him know the danger had passed, and finally tell him he could return home to the loving wife and son that awaited him. Dena, however, held no intentions of allowing him to do so, using the money he sent to fund her second wedding and even going so far as to create a gang of fictional assassins called "The G-Men" that were constantly on the hunt for their prey.

Each time Lee called home, praying that at last the "hunt" had been called off, Dena would insist he stay hidden.

Her current beau, Julian, would not be her only suitor during this time as neighbors would recount other men coming in and out of the home while her husband was away at work. There were even a few close calls in which a visitor would be leaving the home almost at the same time as Julian pulled in for lunch, something he did daily.

Christopher Cordess, a legal adviser on Dena Webb's case, had this to say of her: "She has an enormous ability to project, but this is an intense form of it. It had a sort of psychotic flavor, that is a crazy flavor, so intense that it makes people by some extraordinary mechanism -which I can't explain- has an influence over people that makes them do things which their normal selves would never do or do again."

LIES, LIES AND MORE LIES

Early on in her marriage with Julian, Dena informed her husband that she was terminally ill, and that her employer was threatening to fire her because she had taken so many days away from work due to her sickness.

Julian saw this as outrageous as Dena would look the part, acting weak and lethargic. In reality, however, Dena was being fired because 26,000 pounds were missing from accounts at the Woolwich building society, and she was being investigated for it. She claimed that her first husband, Lee, had returned and had been threatening her, blaming him for the missing money. Dena alleged that her first husband was sending her threatening letters and even secretly recorded him making threatening phone calls to her.

Dena then claimed to her neighbors, the Howells, that Lee had come to her home and raped her. The police took her false accusations seriously, and Lee Wyatt finally became the wanted man he had always wrongly believed he was.

Furious of his situation, Lee returned home whilto confront Dena while Julian was upstairs sleeping. Dena refused to explain anything and managed to turn him away. Little did she know that her web of lies had already begun to fall apart at the seams and her subsequent downfall was imminent.

In 1994, Dena took the final step in her downward spiral of darkness: murder. Detectives believe at this time Julian may have begun to discover the extent of his wife's lies before she took his life with a massive overdose of dothiepin, an anti-depressant, and aspirin hidden in his curry over the course of some days.

Julian loved curry with extra spice, a fact that Dena took advantage of to mask the bitter taste of the poison.

It was on Julian Webb's birthday, June 30th, that his devious wife first informed Julian's mother over the phone that her son had fallen ill and had in fact been sick since Tuesday, two days before.

Dena told his mother that her son had "stayed in the sun too long" and had drunk himself into a stupor, which struck his mother as strange.

She knew that her son didn't partake in alcohol.

Friends and work colleagues of Julian had their suspicions as well, as it was very unlike him to be so sick and to not check in with his loved ones. After his second day of missed work, a male co-worker called to inquire if Julian was okay.

"Oh, well, he's sick," Dena said before hanging up on the man. A number of people called the house inquiring after Julian's health, and each caller would receive a vague, fantastic story as to why he could not come to the phone or work.

At 1:30 a.m. in the morning, on Julian's birthday, Dena would ring the doorbell at the Howell residence, waking them.

She told them that she could not wake up her husband and that he was not breathing. When Dena finally called for help, her husband was long dead and rigid in his bed.

Dena presented the police with two bottles, alleging that her husband had taken an overdose of antidepressants and aspirin on purpose. This was a hard pill for his family to swallow, however, as Julian was a fitness fanatic. He never drank or even took aspirin as he was regimented toward clean living.

"I was awake when the police came 'round to tell me what had happened," Julian's mother recalled. "And I knew as soon as I saw them, before I'd spoken to them, and I heard the police car from upstairs. I just knew."

Julian Webb died of an overdose on his 31st birthday in his bed, at least two hours before an ambulance was called.

Julian's coworkers recall coming up to their work building and finding Dena sitting on the front steps a very short time after his death. She was described as moving between crying and lucidity, and the way she seemed to go between the two so quickly unnerved those that witnessed it. Dena is reported to have said in the same breath, "Julian's dead. I need to speak to someone about the insurance money." To any sane person, these two sentences could not possibly be said in the same conversation, much less the same breath, and yet here was this woman wearing a nightgown and jacket, saying just that.

Dena told the police that her husband committed suicide, but his apparent good health and happy attitude prior to his "sickness" prompted police to investigate. They would discover that the antidepressants belonged not to Julian Webb, but to Dena. Still, the pills were kept in a drawer in the kitchen, where Julian could have easily found and taken them, and thus the fact the pills belonged to Dena held little weight. Though the coroner could not confirm that he had taken the dose accidentally, there was not enough evidence to prove foul play so the medical examiner recorded an open verdict.

Wasting no time, Dena attempted to collect thirty-five thousand pounds from Julian's pension plan which was to be released in the event of his death. Julian's mother would not allow her son's murderer to get away with his life and his money, however, and she was able to quickly establish that Dena was not his next of kin as she was still legally married to her first husband.

Dena also attempted to have Julian's remains cremated, but his family and investigators were able to successfully prevent such an evidence damaging act. It would not be until her trial for attempting to murder her third husband, however, that Julian's body would be exhumed.

The funeral was held at a church on Hayling Island in Northney. Dena Webb showed up wearing a high-riding mini-skirt and a blouse that revealed her ample cleavage.

The right side of the church was packed with friends and family mourning the loss of their Julian, and to the left sat the lone figure of Dena in sexy attire. Friends and colleagues describe Dena's face as emotionless and noticed that the flowers she brought appeared to have been taken from the cemetery nearby.

Much to his family's dismay, Julian's death was eventually ruled an accidental overdose, and Dena Webb moved on in her hunt for a new man to take deadly advantage of.

The freshly widowed Dena looked for love by advertising in the personal ads, describing herself as a "bubbly blonde."

No one proved clever enough to resist her charm. Businessmen, teachers, a prison officer, and even a convicted rapist fell under her ruthless spell before she dumped them or vanished. Detectives believe Dena successfully conned her victims out of a total of a half-million pounds.

One of her victims, Robert Waite, was found and interviewed. He had worked with Dena in 1980 and, years later, suddenly received a card from her inviting him to a reunion party. He called her, and Dena invited him to dinner then seduced him.

Dena would tell Waite that Julian had died from an overdose of steroids and that her first husband, Lee Wyatt, had beaten and attacked her regularly. Waite believed her, as he had no reason not to. But when Mr. Waite began to pull away out of disinterest, Dena quickly convinced him that she was dying of a terminal illness. Wishing to help a dying woman, he promised to take her to one of her favorite places, Florida, to care for her during her last months of life. After they arrived, while the two were lying in bed at a motel, Waite woke to feel a sharp prick in his side. He became entirely sure that Dena drugged him and slept through an entire day.

Soon after, Dena left him for broke, saying she had to appear as a witness in an anti-mafia trial in New York. She was actually flying back to Britain as she was due to appear in court for defrauding the Woolwich. For three weeks, Waite was stranded. Evenually, he came back to England and on August 31st, 1995 he discovered that Dena Webb had just been convicted of fraud and sent to jail. It was revealed during this trial that Dena had falsified the alleged death threats sent to her by mail from Lee Wyatt, and even his recorded calls were scripted by her. At the time of their creation, Lee believed that he was creating them to protect his family. The police were able to conclude that Lee was in fact hundreds of miles away during the time of the thefts working in Newquay under an assumed identity, and the charges against him were dropped. Dena was released after only nine months, and she soon returned home.

A NEW MAN, ANOTHER SUCKER

Richard Thompson was just another name on the long list of pockets Dena wished to empty when he discovered her personal ad in a Lonely Hearts column. The two met and "hit it off", marrying in a Holiday Inn in Florida.

The two were forced to round up strangers, one of which was the manager of the hotel, as witnesses after Dena's supposed "friends and family" did not show.

Thompson had money and owned a home in an affluent community which Dena found to her liking. She lied and charmed Thompson, claiming a love of deep-sea fishing which was his favorite hobby.

Dena told Richard that she had won the lottery and could access the money in the States, and so the loving couple made plans to travel overseas and claim her winnings. After the trip had been finalized, Dena enthralled her new husband with ideas of becoming

"a big game ocean skipper" and opening a fishing company.

This inspired Richard to attend classes run by the U.S. Coast Guard. He passed his boating exam, a feat that did not come without a huge amount of hard work. Richard then took an early retirement, and his wife used the money to renovate his cottage in order to rent it out while they were away in Florida building their new life. The new Mrs. Dena Thompson then suggested they combine their financial assets, a suggestion that the blissfully in love Richard saw as a reasonable thing to do. He even made out his will to his wife, giving her power of attorney over his financial affairs. Not long after this, Dena allegedly asked him if their waste disposal unit might be powerful enough to crush bones. A chilling question, to be sure, but a question that Richard thought little about.

Unfortunately for Richard, his wife had a murderous surprise in store for him just one day before the couple were to leave for the States.

On that fateful night, according to Richard's testimony, his wife had promised him a wild round of rough, kinky sex which was something he eagerly accepted.

Before getting ready, Dena locked their German Shepard, Oden, away in another room. She then informed her husband that a man would be coming the following day with a green card for him, which he would then be able to use to go to Florida.

She then started to run a hot bath and told him to "get ready for some fun."

With her husband anticipating something kinky, he allowed Dena to tie up his hands and feet.

"Get ready for a night to remember," she cooed, placing a towel over his face.

Dena then picked up a baseball bat and cracked it over his head.

Once then twice for good measure.

Stunned with blood pouring into his eyes, Richard jerked and twisted his body enough to loosen the restraints on his wrists. He sat up but Dena was ready for him.

Grabbing a butcher knife from the night stand beside their bed, she stabbed him in the shoulder. Still dazed from the baseball bat hits to the head, Richard miraculously recovered and pushed Dena away.

Dena slipped on his blood on the floor. Richard seized the advantage, pushing his thumb into her eye. Dena went for the knife again but Richard pushed harder with his thumb.

"I'll put your eye through your head if you don't let go of the knife," Richard warned.

THE AFTERMATH

It would be several days after Richard fought for and won his life that the idea to check his bank accounts would suddenly come to him. A quick call had his accountant checking his assets, and sure enough, it was discovered that Dena, the woman he had grown to love, had cleaned out his bank accounts. She also made inquiries about surrendering his 89,000 pound life insurance policy and put up his house for sale without his knowledge.

"I fell for her personality," Richard said afterward. "I trusted her 100 percent."

Dena was put on trial for attempted murder and fraud, with Richard as the key witness.

She would plead not guilty and her attorney claimed it was Richard who attacked his wife, becoming violent when she told him that Florida had all been a lie, and that Dena had hit him with the bat in self-defense.

The jury fell for Dena's charm as well, acquitting her of attempted murder.

The district attorney would call the case his "the most staggering court verdict I ever had."

Dena was, however, sentenced to three years and nine months at Lewes Crown Court on fifteen counts of fraud, involving thousands of pounds that she stole from her husband Richard, as well as two other lovers. Not only had Richard been nearly murdered without warning, but now he was financially bankrupt and emotionally devastated. During the trial, Dena admitted that her husband was not the only one she had defrauded, and she was convicted to eighteen months in jail for stealing 26,000 pounds from her old employer, the Woolwich building society, by setting up fake accounts. She had also stolen 5,000 pounds from a former boyfriend.

"I had never seen such a miscarriage of justice," Richard said. "It was appalling."

Dissatisfied with the outcome of the trial, the police began an investigation into Dena's past and quickly discovered some disturbingly repetitive facts. They discovered a long train of men left destitute in the wake of the "bubbly blonde" that promised them love and companionship. They also took a second look at the fate of her late husband, Julian Webb, and the cruel lies that sent Lee Wyatt into homelessness for three years. Immediately following their discovery of Julian Webb's death and the investigation into Dena regarding his overdose, investigators reopened the case and exhumed Julian Webb's body for further examination. For six years, Dena Thompson had gotten away with murder, but the attack on her current husband would prove to be her undoing.

Forensic scientists confirmed that antidepressants caused his death, but concluded that the medication was administered over a period of time rather than all at once. This ruled out Dena's original claim of suicide and made it clear that Julian had in fact been poisoned over the course of a week. Scientists were able to prove this by examining his stomach and blood content. The last days of Julian Webb's life would have been horrific. Isolated from his friends and family, Julian would lie dying in his bed, knowing something was wrong but unable to help himself or reach out to others. All the while, Dena nursed him, likely feeding him by hand in what must have appeared to be an act of love and devotion. Instead, this monstrous psychopath was dosing him with still more and more antidepressants and aspirin.

Julian's final moments would have been filled with agony as his body shut down, with Dena's emotionless face being the last thing he would ever see.

Nine years after his untimely demise, Julian Webb's killer would finally be brought to justice. In 2003, Dena Thompson received life, with a minimum of sixteen years, for murder.

FINALLY...

Dena Thompson was a master manipulator of people, with one husband murdered, another almost murdered, and a third on the run and penniless.

The Recorder of London, Michael Hyam, is quoted saying to Mrs. Thompson that her crimes were "utterly ruthless and without any pity. Nothing can excuse you for the wickedness of what you did."

Immediately after the conviction, UK investigators put together a large scale search for any and all of Mrs. Thompson's previous victims with the fear that they had a serial killer on their hands. The search took investigators and Interpol across the length of Europe to Bulgaria, where Dena had been a regular visitor throughout the late 1970s and early 1980s. One Bulgarian boyfriend by the name of Stoyan Kostov was never found, and the fear is that he was an early victim of Dena who was no referred to as the "Black Widow." How did she make her way to Bulgaria?

Dena was an avid gymnast at a young age, although she never chose to compete, and her father, Michael Holmes, was highly involved in the sport. This is allegedly how Mrs. Thompson's Bulgarian connections were made.

Inspector Martyn Underhill felt a certain sense of urgency when searching for Mr. Kostov (last known address: 27 K.D. Avramov Street, Svishtov), but was unable to find the man.

"We cannot rule out the possibility that other partners have been injured in some way," Inspector Underhill said.

Dena visited Bulgaria for several years, with her gymnastics connections said to be her reason. Much mystery hangs over these visits and the still missing Kostov, and it is suggested that Dena's murderous ways began long before she ever met Julian Webb. If Kostov is indeed Dena Thompson's first victim, he could be the only person on earth capable of shedding light on what turned Dena towards a life of crime.

The investigation came to an eventual end, however, when no solid evidence could be found on any murders prior to Julian Webb. Some, including a UK journalist named Adrian Gatton, believe that there is much more to the Bulgarian story than could be found by police. It is suggested that the operation carried out by Interpol and West Yorkshire police was done half-heartedly, as they may never have visited Bulgaria.

There are likely many unnamed men made victims by Dena Thompson's grandiose lies, but they might feel too embarrassed to come forward and identify themselves. It is proven that she stole from a dozen different men, but police believe the number to be much larger. Dena Thompson maintains her innocence, and her most recent appeal against conviction has failed.

In 2007, she was sentenced to a minimum of sixteen years in prison.